NORTH CAROLINA TEST PREP

Writing Skills Workbook

Guided Practice

Grade 5

ISBN 978-1729363898

TEST MASTER PRESS

www.testmasterpress.com

CONTENTS

INTRODUCTION
For Parents, Teachers, and Tutors

Developing Writing Skills

Student learning in North Carolina is based on the skills described in the *North Carolina Standard Course of Study*. These standards were introduced in 2017, and fully implemented in the 2018-2019 school year. The standards describe what students are expected to know. This workbook is specifically designed to develop the writing skills described in the standards. Students will write in response to passages, as well as write narratives, persuasive texts, and essays. Students will gain experience completing research projects and edit and revise their work. While the workbook is mainly focused on writing skills, students will also develop strong reading skills as they provide written answers to reading comprehension questions.

Completing Practice Sets

This workbook is divided into 10 practice sets. Each practice set includes four tasks that progress from simple to more complex. The types of tasks are described below.

Task Type	Details
Short Passage with Questions	These tasks contain a short passage followed by reading comprehension questions requiring written answers. They also include a Core Skills Practice exercise that focuses on one key writing, reading, or language skill. These exercises may require students to respond to a text, complete a research project, or complete a writing task.
Long Passage with Essay Question	These tasks contain a long passage followed by an essay question requiring a written answer of 1 to 2 pages. They also include hints and planning guidance to help students develop effective writing skills.
Personal Narrative Writing Task	These tasks contain a writing prompt for a personal narrative, as well as hints and planning guidance.
Short Story Writing Task	These tasks contain a writing prompt for a story, as well as hints and planning guidance.
Opinion Piece Writing Task	These tasks contain a writing prompt for an opinion piece, as well as hints and planning guidance.
Explanatory Writing Task	These tasks contain a writing prompt for an essay, as well as hints and planning guidance.

By completing the practice sets, students will have experience with all types of writing tasks. This includes writing in response to passages, writing all the types of texts covered in the state standards, gathering information from sources, and completing research projects. Some of the writing tasks also include guides for editing and revising completed work. This encourages students to review their work and improve on it, while the checklists help ensure that students focus on the key criteria that work is judged on.

Preparing for the End-of-Grade English Language Arts/Reading Assessments

The End-of-Grade ELA/Reading tests assess reading skills by having students read literary and informational passages and answer multiple choice questions about the passages. This book will help prepare students for the tests by improving reading comprehension skills. The questions and exercises will develop advanced reading comprehension skills and give students ongoing practice analyzing texts. This will ensure that students have the skills needed to excel on the test.

Reading and Writing

Practice Set 1

This practice set contains four writing tasks. These are described below.

Task 1: Short Passage with Questions

This task has a short passage followed by questions. Read each question carefully. Then write your answer in the space provided.

You can also practice writing skills by completing the Core Skills Practice exercise.

Task 2: Short Passage with Questions

This task has a short passage followed by questions. Read each question carefully. Then write your answer in the space provided.

You can also practice writing skills by completing the Core Skills Practice exercise.

Task 3: Long Passage with Essay Question

This task has a longer passage with an essay question. Read the passage, complete the planning page, and then write or type your answer.

Task 4: Personal Narrative Writing Task

This final task requires you to write a personal narrative. Read the writing prompt, complete the planning page, and then write or type your answer.

Task 1: Short Passage with Questions

Mozart

Mozart is a famous German composer of the classical era. He is also known as Wolfgang Amadeus Mozart. He has composed over 600 pieces of classical music. These include works for the piano and violin, as well as whole operas.

Mozart began composing at the age of 5. At this time, he wrote small pieces for his father. He continued to learn and write music all through his youth. When he was 17, he worked as a court musician in Austria. He was given the opportunity to write a range of musical pieces. Mozart left Austria in search of better work, and lived in Paris for over a year. During this time, he was unable to find work, but he still continued writing music. He then moved to Vienna. Mozart wrote most of his best-known work while living in Vienna. He died at the age of 35 in 1791.

CORE SKILLS PRACTICE
WRITE A RESEARCH REPORT

Mozart was one famous composer during the classical era. Another famous composer was Ludwig van Beethoven. Research and write a short report about Ludwig van Beethoven. Use the questions below to guide your research.

Where and when was Beethoven born?

Where did Beethoven live during his life?

What music did Beethoven write?

What are some of Beethoven's best-known works?

What influence did Beethoven's music have?

1 Mozart can be described as gifted. Give **three** details that show that Mozart was gifted.

1: ____

____

2: ____

____

3: ____

____

2 Complete the chart below by describing **two** places that Mozart lived after Austria and what he did in each place.

Place	Details
Austria	Worked as a court musician

Task 2: Short Passage with Questions

Clowns

Mickey didn't like clowns. When his family told him that he would be going to the circus, he was excited. He knew there would be lions, camels, and a trapeze artist. Then he remembered that there would also be clowns. He became very nervous.

"Don't worry," said his father. "You'll be fine. Your mother and I will be with you."

Mickey felt a little better and decided to go. He took his seat in the front row of the audience. The trapeze artists performed first, and Mickey was amazed by their skill. After a short break, it was time for the clowns. As the clowns came out onto the stage, Mickey froze. He thought about running off, even though he wasn't really sure what he was afraid of. But he sat quietly in his seat reminding himself over and over that there was nothing to fear.

Gradually, his feelings of fear faded away. He started to smile as the clowns pranced around. By the time the performance was over, Mickey was giggling along with everyone else in the audience.

CORE SKILLS PRACTICE

Compare how Mickey feels about clowns at the start and the end of the passage.

____

____

____

____

____

1 What is Mickey's main problem? How does he overcome his problem?

____

____

____

____

____

____

2 In the last paragraph, what does the word "pranced" suggest about the clowns?

Hint This question is asking you to think about more than just the dictionary meaning of the word. Think about what image it creates, or how it makes you feel.

____

____

____

____

____

____

Task 3: Long Passage with Essay Question

Directions: Read the passage below. Then answer the question that follows. Use the planning page to plan your writing. Then write or type your essay.

Grooming a King Charles Cavalier

The King Charles Cavalier is a small breed of Spaniel dog. It is known as a toy dog by kennel clubs. They are very popular in the United States and around the world. These dogs have a silky coat and can be difficult to groom. Professional groomers can carry out the task. However, many owners choose to save money and groom their dog themselves. It takes some patience, but you can learn to groom a King Charles Cavalier.

Start by making sure you have the correct equipment to groom your dog correctly. You will need:

- a comb
- a brush
- dog-friendly conditioner

You should complete these steps when your dog is clean. If your dog's coat is dirty, give the dog a bath first. Then dry the coat before starting.

Step 1

Before you start, make sure that your dog is in a comfortable position either on your lap or on a blanket. Your dog should be nice and relaxed.

Step 2

Take your comb and move it smoothly through the coat. There may be some knots or tangles, so be sure not to comb it too fast. You don't want to pull at the dog's fur, cause your dog any discomfort, or scare it. Be gentle, but make sure that all dead or matted hair is removed.

Step 3
Once the combing is complete, add some of the conditioner to the coat. This will add shine and make it easier to brush your dog.

Step 4
Comb your dog's coat for a second time to make sure that it is as smooth as it can be.

Step 5
It is now time to brush your King Charles Cavalier. Hold the brush firmly in your hand and be sure to keep your dog still. Move the brush gently through your dog's coat. Take care to smooth out any lumps or patches of uneven hair. Move through each area of the coat twice.

Step 6
Once you've finished brushing, condition your dogs coat again. This helps to keep your dog's coat free from tangles. It will also make it easier to groom your dog in the future.

Step 7
Lastly, all you need to do is gently pat the dog's coat dry. Your dog is now nicely groomed and the coat should stay that way for around 4 to 6 weeks.

You can give your dog a small food reward after you've finished the grooming. This will help make sure your dog looks forward to being groomed.

1 Do you think it would be easy to groom a King Charles Cavalier? What do you think it would be most important to do when grooming the dog to make it easier? Use details from the passage in your answer.

In your answer, be sure to

- describe whether or not it would be easy to groom a King Charles Cavalier
- explain what you think it would be most important to do when grooming the dog to make it easier
- use details from the passage in your answer
- write an answer of between 1 and 2 pages

The passage gives advice on how to groom a King Charles Cavalier. Start your answer by describing whether or not you think it would be easy to groom the dog. Then describe ways that you could make it easier. You should use the advice given in the passage when answering this part of the question.

Planning Page

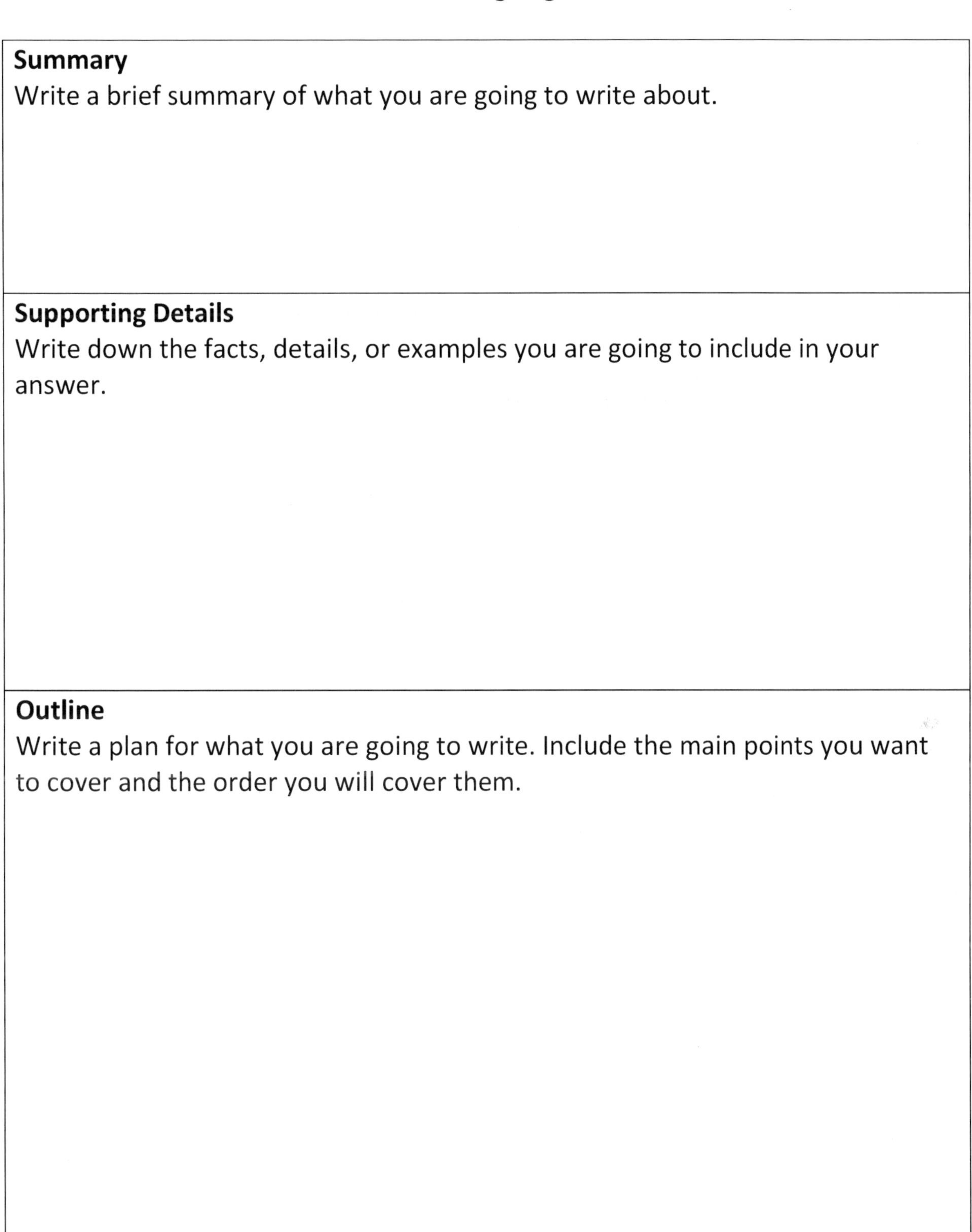

Summary

Write a brief summary of what you are going to write about.

Supporting Details

Write down the facts, details, or examples you are going to include in your answer.

Outline

Write a plan for what you are going to write. Include the main points you want to cover and the order you will cover them.

Task 4: Personal Narrative Writing Task

Directions: Read the writing prompt below. Use the planning page to plan your writing. Then write or type your answer.

Everyone needs help sometimes. Think about a time when you needed help. Who did you ask for help and how did the person help you?

Write a composition describing a time when you asked someone for help. Describe why you asked for help, who you asked for help, and what happened in the end.

Hint

Make sure you answer each part of the question. Remember that you need to include the following:

- why you asked for help
- who you asked for help
- what happened when you asked for help

When you write your outline, make sure that it covers all of the parts of the question.

Planning Page

Summary

Write a brief summary of what you are going to write about.

Outline

Write a plan for what you are going to write. Include the main points you want to cover and the order you will cover them.

Writing and Editing Checklist

After you finish writing your personal narrative, you can use this guide to review and edit your work. Use the questions as a guide to finding ways you can improve your work.

Writing Checklist

- ✓ Does your work have a strong opening? Does it introduce the main ideas or set the scene well?
- ✓ Is your work well-organized? Is related information grouped together? Does each paragraph have one main idea?
- ✓ Does your work have an effective ending? Does it tie up the events well?
- ✓ Is your work focused? Are there any details that do not fit with your main ideas?
- ✓ Do your ideas flow well? Have you used words and phrases to link ideas well?
- ✓ Have you used strong words? Are there words that could be replaced with better ones?
- ✓ Have you used effective descriptions? Could your descriptions be improved?
- ✓ Have you used sensory details? Could you add more sensory details to help readers imagine the scene?

Editing Checklist

- ✓ Have you used a variety of sentence structures? Are your sentences all written correctly?
- ✓ Is the grammar correct?
- ✓ Are all words spelled correctly? You can check the spelling of any words you are not sure of.
- ✓ Is punctuation used correctly?
- ✓ If dialogue is used, is it punctuated correctly?
- ✓ Are all words capitalized correctly?

Reading and Writing

Practice Set 2

This practice set contains four writing tasks. These are described below.

Task 1: Short Passage with Questions

This task has a short passage followed by questions. Read each question carefully. Then write your answer in the space provided.

You can also practice writing skills by completing the Core Skills Practice exercise.

Task 2: Short Passage with Questions

This task has a short passage followed by questions. Read each question carefully. Then write your answer in the space provided.

You can also practice writing skills by completing the Core Skills Practice exercise.

Task 3: Short Story Writing Task

This task requires you to write a short story. Read the writing prompt, complete the planning page, and then write or type your answer.

Task 4: Opinion Piece Writing Task

This final task requires you to write an opinion piece. Read the writing prompt, complete the planning page, and then write or type your answer.

Task 1: Short Passage with Questions

Raindrops

It is a popular belief that rain falls in droplets shaped like teardrops. Raindrops are often drawn to look this way. If you've ever watched a weather report on the news, you might have seen symbols representing rainfall. The raindrops are often shown as if they are teardrops. This is a nice idea, but not a practical one.

Raindrops are actually spherical rather than teardrop-shaped. This is a common property of falling liquid. Raindrops also change shape depending on how they are falling. If they are falling fast, the bottom might be pushed up. The top will then stay rounded, but the bottom will be pushed flat. The shape is a little like the top of a mushroom.

CORE SKILLS PRACTICE

The passage has two paragraphs. Describe the main purpose of each paragraph. Include how each paragraph relates to the overall purpose of the passage.

Paragraph 1: ____

____

____

Paragraph 2: ____

____

____

1 What is the main purpose of the diagram?

Hint To answer this question, you should explain what the diagram shows and how it relates to the information in the passage.

____

____

____

____

____

____

2 Compare the actual shape of raindrops with the shape that many people think they are.

____

____

____

____

____

____

Task 2: Short Passage with Questions

Dearest Donna

One year together, one year of bliss,
You brighten my days with your tender kiss.
I hope that you'll be my sweet valentine,
And say that you will always be mine.

In the future we may well get married,
On the wings of love we'll be carried.
As we grow old as one and together,
Side by side as partners forever.

CORE SKILLS PRACTICE
WRITE A POEM

This poem is a rhyming poem. One common rhyme pattern is to have the second and fourth lines of a poem rhyme. Here is an example of this rhyme pattern:

It was a dark and stormy night.
There was a huge thunder crash.
Into my room and under my bed,
the poor little cat did dash.

Choose a pair of rhyming words from the list below. Use the words to write a poem with four lines where the second and fourth lines rhyme.

street	beat	eat	seat	sweet
meet	greet	treat	sleet	cheat

1 Describe the rhyme pattern of the poem "Dearest Donna."

2 Who is the speaker addressing the poem to? Explain how you can tell.

Hint Think about how the speaker uses the words "you" and "we" in the poem. The title of the poem is also important.

Task 3: Short Story Writing Task

Directions: Read the writing prompt below. Use the planning page to plan your writing. Then write or type your answer.

Shane walked into the classroom and took his seat. Then Miss Marvin walked in. She was the strangest teacher that Shane had ever seen. And she was about to teach the strangest class ever.

Write a story about the class that Miss Marvin teaches.

Hint

The writing prompt tells you that your story should be about the class that Miss Marvin teaches, and it tells you that the class should be strange. Use this as the starting point and think of a story based around this idea. You can decide what is strange about the class. Use your imagination and come up with a clear idea about what happens that is strange. Then use your story to describe what happens. Be creative and try to make your story interesting!

Planning Page

The Story
Write a summary of your story.

The Beginning
Describe what is going to happen at the start of your story.

The Middle
Describe what is going to happen in the middle of your story.

The End
Describe what is going to happen at the end of your story.

Task 4: Opinion Piece Writing Task

Directions: Read the writing prompt below. Use the planning page to plan your writing. Then write or type your answer.

Getting Things Done

I have a plan for tomorrow.
I have a plan for today.
As long as I stick to my plans,
nothing ever gets in my way.

In "Getting Things Done," the poet describes how he gets things done by planning. Do you think it is important to plan? Why or why not? Write a composition describing why it is important to plan, or why planning is unimportant.

Hint

You may have several different opinions. Maybe you think planning can sometimes be helpful, but that too much planning can make life boring. A good composition will have one clear idea. Even if you have several ideas, choose one to focus on in your writing. It is better to support one opinion very well than to describe many different opinions!

Planning Page

Summary
Write a brief summary of what you are going to write about.

Supporting Details
Write down the facts, details, or examples you are going to include.

Outline
Write a plan for what you are going to write. Include the main points you want to cover and the order you will cover them.

Writing and Editing Checklist

After you finish writing your opinion piece, you can use this guide to review and edit your work. Use the questions as a guide to finding ways you can improve your work.

Writing Checklist

- ✓ Does your work have one clear opinion?
- ✓ Does your work have a strong opening? Does the opening introduce the topic and state the opinion?
- ✓ Is your opinion supported? Have you used facts, details, and examples to support your opinion?
- ✓ Is your work well-organized? Is related information grouped together? Does each paragraph have one main idea?
- ✓ Do your ideas flow well? Have you used words and phrases to link ideas well?
- ✓ Does your work have a strong ending? Does the ending restate the main idea and tie up the opinion piece?

Editing Checklist

- ✓ Have you used a variety of sentence structures? Are your sentences all written correctly?
- ✓ Is the grammar correct?
- ✓ Are all words spelled correctly? You can check the spelling of any words you are not sure of.
- ✓ Is punctuation used correctly?
- ✓ If dialogue is used, is it punctuated correctly?
- ✓ Are all words capitalized correctly?

Reading and Writing

Practice Set 3

This practice set contains four writing tasks. These are described below.

Task 1: Short Passage with Questions

This task has a short passage followed by questions. Read each question carefully. Then write your answer in the space provided.

You can also practice writing skills by completing the Core Skills Practice exercise.

Task 2: Short Passage with Questions

This task has a short passage followed by questions. Read each question carefully. Then write your answer in the space provided.

You can also practice writing skills by completing the Core Skills Practice exercise.

Task 3: Long Passage with Essay Question

This task has a longer passage with an essay question. Read the passage, complete the planning page, and then write or type your answer.

Task 4: Personal Narrative Writing Task

This final task requires you to write a personal narrative. Read the writing prompt, complete the planning page, and then write or type your answer.

Task 1: Short Passage with Questions

Something Special

Toby had played basketball for the school since he was eleven. When he reached sixteen, he was dropped from the team because his coach said he was too short. Toby was upset, but his father told him not to give up.

Toby played on the weekend with his friends. After school, he played by himself. Without anyone else to play with, he spent a lot of time learning ball skills. He enjoyed learning to do new things with the ball. But he missed playing in real games and being part of a team.

When they moved the following year, Toby trained with his new school team. His coach was impressed with his ball skills. Toby was delighted to be selected for the team. He later became the star player for his new team.

CORE SKILLS PRACTICE
WRITE A PERSUASIVE LETTER

Imagine that you are Toby. You have just been dropped from the team and want to write a letter to your coach. You want to persuade your coach to let you play on the team again. List **three** reasons your coach should let you play below. Then write a persuasive letter to your coach using these reasons.

1. ____

____

2. ____

____

3. ____

____

1 Use information from the passage to complete the table below.

Ways that Toby Keeps Playing Basketball After He is Dropped from the School Team
1)
2)

2 How does Toby being dropped from the school team lead to his later success?

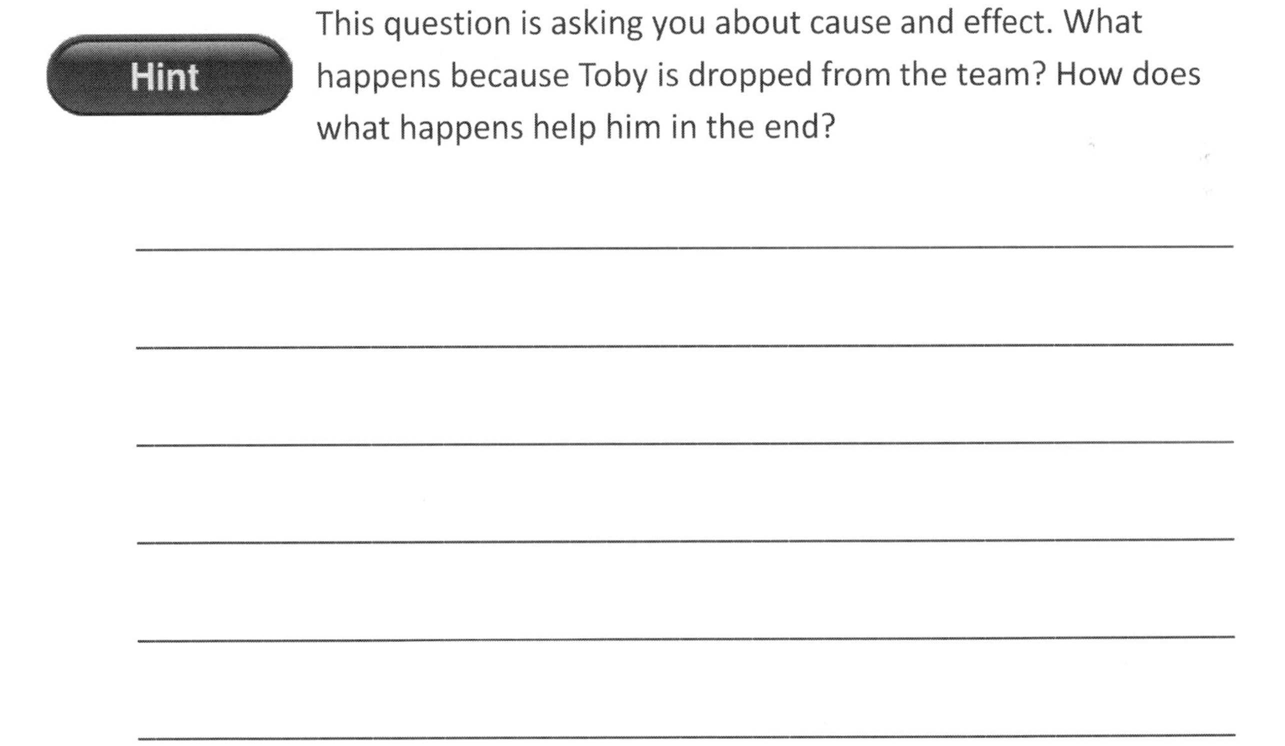

This question is asking you about cause and effect. What happens because Toby is dropped from the team? How does what happens help him in the end?

Task 2: Short Passage with Questions

Penny's Powers

Penny was a beautiful princess. She lived in a tall towering castle that almost reached the clouds. What people didn't know was that she had special wishing powers. But Penny often failed to use them because she had everything she had ever wanted. She had no need to wish for food, or pretty things, or happy times. Every day was pleasant for Penny, so she assumed that every day was pleasant for other people as well.

One day, a poor man visited her and asked for help. He explained that he had lost his crops and his home in a terrible storm. He spent every day out searching for enough food to feed his family, and his poor wife often had to search for food too. He said he would do anything to be able to provide for his family again. Penny agreed to help him right away. She used her powers to wish that the man's land and home would be returned to new. Penny was shocked by how pleased the man was. He jumped up and down, clapped his hands, and a tear even rolled down his cheek. She had never realized how lucky she was. From that day forward, she decided to use her powers to help as many people as she could.

CORE SKILLS PRACTICE

Think about why Penny doesn't use her powers until she meets the poor man. Is it selfish of Penny not to use her powers? Explain your answer.

____

____

____

____

____

1 How can you tell that the events in the passage could not really happen?

Hint The events in the passage are made-up and could not happen in real life. Explain how you can tell this.

2 Identify the hyperbole in the first paragraph and explain why the author used it.

Hint Hyperbole is a literary technique where exaggeration is used to make a point or emphasize the qualities of something.

3 How does Penny change in the passage? What causes Penny to change? Use details from the passage in your answer.

Hint

To answer this question, start by describing what Penny is like at the start of the passage. Then describe what makes her change. Finish by explaining how she has changed.

Task 3: Long Passage with Essay Question

Directions: Read the passage below. Then answer the question that follows. Use the planning page to plan your writing. Then write or type your essay.

The Girlfriend and the Mother

Prince Arnold had a very close bond with his mother. They shared everything with each other. They had remained close since he had been a child. One day, he met a girl named Chloe and she became his girlfriend. Gradually, Arnold began to spend more time with his girlfriend than with his mother.

Although he still enjoyed long conversations with his mother, she began to feel left out. She felt that the only time she would get to spend with him was in the evenings. This was when he would fall asleep on the couch and she would sit beside him and stroke his hair.

His mother really liked the gray strands that grew in his hair. She felt they made him look wise. So as she stroked his head she would remove some of the darker hairs from his scalp. She did this over many nights for an entire year.

Arnold's girlfriend had a similar habit. She thought that his gray hairs made him look old. So she would pluck as many gray hairs from his head as she possibly could. She too did this for many nights over the year.

After a year had gone by, Arnold found that he was almost completely bald. His mother and girlfriend had removed so much of his hair that he was left only with short little tufts. Both women and Arnold were unhappy with his new look. The ladies felt that their battle for his time had led to the problem.

"We're so sorry," they said. "What we have done is unfair."

They realized that they must all get along and spend time together if they were to remain happy. The mother and the girlfriend made a promise to be happy sharing Prince Arnold's time.

1 Explain why Prince Arnold loses his hair. Include how both his mother and girlfriend cause him to lose his hair. Use details from the passage in your answer.

In your answer, be sure to
- explain why Prince Arnold loses his hair
- describe the role that his girlfriend plays
- describe the role that his mother plays
- use details from the passage in your answer
- write an answer of between 1 and 2 pages

This question has several parts. It is important to answer all parts. As you plan your writing, make sure you are answering all parts.

When you write your outline, you can divide what you are going to write into paragraphs. In the first paragraph, you might describe why Prince Arnold loses his hair overall. In the second paragraph, you can describe the role that his girlfriend plays in detail. In the third paragraph, you can describe the role that his mother plays in detail. In the fourth paragraph, you can summarize what you have written.

Planning Page

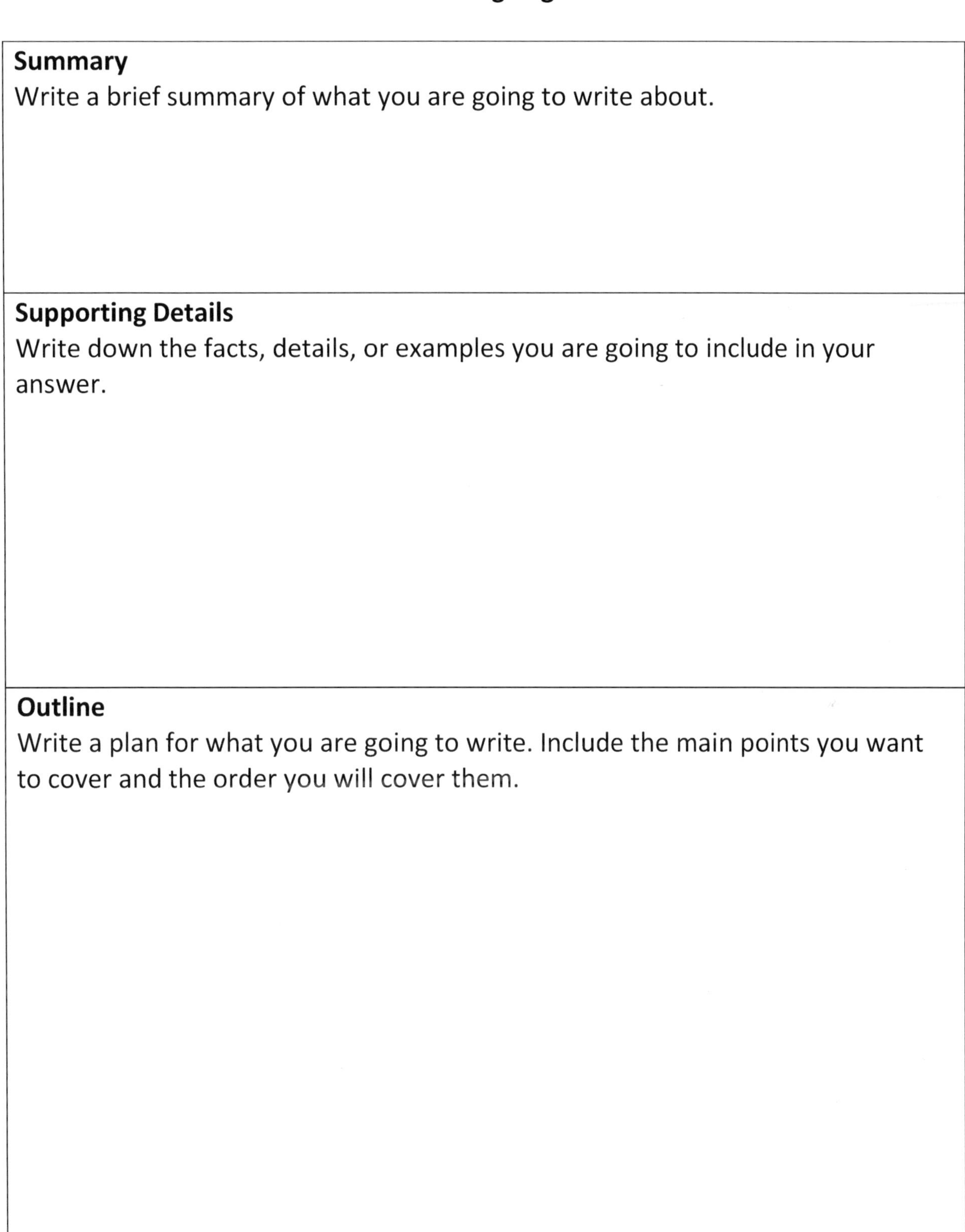

Summary
Write a brief summary of what you are going to write about.

Supporting Details
Write down the facts, details, or examples you are going to include in your answer.

Outline
Write a plan for what you are going to write. Include the main points you want to cover and the order you will cover them.

Task 4: Personal Narrative Writing Task

Directions: Read the writing prompt below. Use the planning page to plan your writing. Then write or type your answer.

It feels good to do something that you are proud of. Think about a time when you did something that you were proud of.

Write a composition describing a time when you did something that you were proud of. Explain what you did and why you felt proud.

Hint

Stay focused! You might be able to think of many different times you could write about, but don't try to write about them all. Instead, choose just one time and write about that time in detail.

Your answer should describe what you did that you were proud of. You should include details that will help the reader imagine what you did and why you felt proud of it. When choosing which details to include, ask yourself whether the detail helps explain why you felt proud. For example, you might be proud because you achieved something that was difficult for you. It would then be relevant to explain why it was difficult for you.

Planning Page

Summary

Write a brief summary of what you are going to write about.

Outline

Write a plan for what you are going to write. Include the main points you want to cover and the order you will cover them.

Writing and Editing Checklist

After you finish writing your personal narrative, you can use this guide to review and edit your work. Use the questions as a guide to finding ways you can improve your work.

Writing Checklist

- ✓ Does your work have a strong opening? Does it introduce the main ideas or set the scene well?
- ✓ Is your work well-organized? Is related information grouped together? Does each paragraph have one main idea?
- ✓ Does your work have an effective ending? Does it tie up the events well?
- ✓ Is your work focused? Are there any details that do not fit with your main ideas?
- ✓ Do your ideas flow well? Have you used words and phrases to link ideas well?
- ✓ Have you used strong words? Are there words that could be replaced with better ones?
- ✓ Have you used effective descriptions? Could your descriptions be improved?
- ✓ Have you used sensory details? Could you add more sensory details to help readers imagine the scene?

Editing Checklist

- ✓ Have you used a variety of sentence structures? Are your sentences all written correctly?
- ✓ Is the grammar correct?
- ✓ Are all words spelled correctly? You can check the spelling of any words you are not sure of.
- ✓ Is punctuation used correctly?
- ✓ If dialogue is used, is it punctuated correctly?
- ✓ Are all words capitalized correctly?

Reading and Writing

Practice Set 4

This practice set contains four writing tasks. These are described below.

Task 1: Short Passage with Questions

This task has a short passage followed by questions. Read each question carefully. Then write your answer in the space provided.

You can also practice writing skills by completing the Core Skills Practice exercise.

Task 2: Short Passage with Questions

This task has a short passage followed by questions. Read each question carefully. Then write your answer in the space provided.

You can also practice writing skills by completing the Core Skills Practice exercise.

Task 3: Opinion Piece Writing Task

This task requires you to write an opinion piece. Read the writing prompt, complete the planning page, and then write or type your answer.

Task 4: Short Story Writing Task

This task requires you to write a short story. Read the writing prompt, complete the planning page, and then write or type your answer.

Task 1: Short Passage with Questions

Brain Size

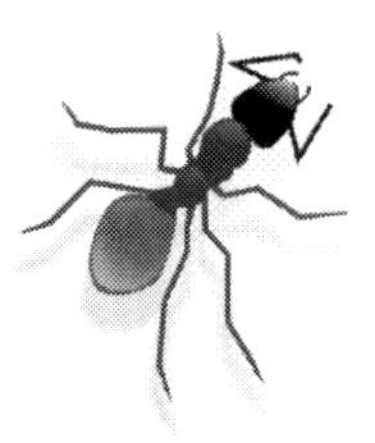

Did you know that the common ant has the largest brain in relation to its size? The brain of an ant is 6 percent of its total body weight. The average human brain is just over 2 percent of a person's body weight.

A single ant brain has a fraction of the ability of a human one. But a colony of ants may have just as much ability. An average nest has 40,000 ants. In total, these ants would have about the same number of brain cells as a person. Ants really are fascinating little creatures.

CORE SKILLS PRACTICE

Ants often work together. To do this, they have to communicate with each other. Research and write a short description of how ants communicate.

____

____

____

____

____

____

____

____

1 Why do you think the author starts the passage with a question?

Hint To answer this question, think about the author's purpose. How does starting with a question affect readers?

____

____

____

____

____

____

2 Describe **three** facts given about ants.

Hint A fact is something that can be proven to be true.

1: ____

____

2: ____

____

3: ____

____

Task 2: Short Passage with Questions

Mosquitoes

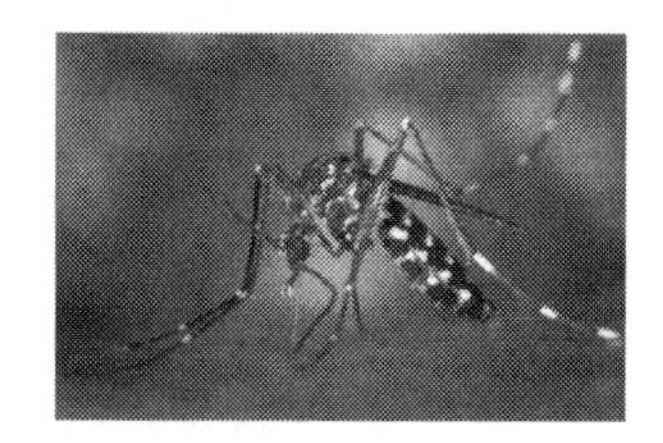

It is well known that mosquitoes carry disease. But did you know that only females bite humans? Male mosquitoes only bite plants and greenery. Both genders carry over 100 separate diseases. It is the female of the species though, that passes these diseases onto people.

It was only in 1877 that British doctor Patrick Manson first discovered that mosquitoes could be very dangerous creatures.

CORE SKILLS PRACTICE

There are many diseases that are spread by mosquitoes. Use the Internet to find out the names of some diseases that are passed onto people by mosquitoes. Complete the list below by adding four more diseases that are spread by mosquitoes.

1. *Malaria*
2. ____________________
3. ____________________
4. ____________________
5. ____________________

1 If the author added another sentence to the end of the article, what do you think it would describe?

____

____

____

____

____

____

2 Describe **one** way that male and female mosquitoes are similar. Describe **one** way that male and female mosquitoes are different.

Hint Make sure you use information from the passage when identifying similarities and differences.

____

____

____

____

____

____

Task 3: Opinion Piece Writing Task

Directions: Read the writing prompt below. Use the planning page to plan your writing. Then write or type your answer.

Imagine that your cousin lives in another state. You want your cousin to come and stay at your home for a few weeks.

Write a letter to your cousin to persuade him or her to visit. Use reasons, facts, or details to persuade your cousin.

Hint

The writing prompt describes the purpose of your writing. In this case, you want to persuade someone to come and stay with you. You will need to give reasons that will help make your cousin want to stay with you. Think of two or three good reasons to use in your letter.

It is also important to think about who the audience is. This will impact the writing style that you use. You are writing this letter to your cousin. A letter to a cousin does not have to be formal or serious. You can write it in a casual way as if you are writing to a friend.

Planning Page

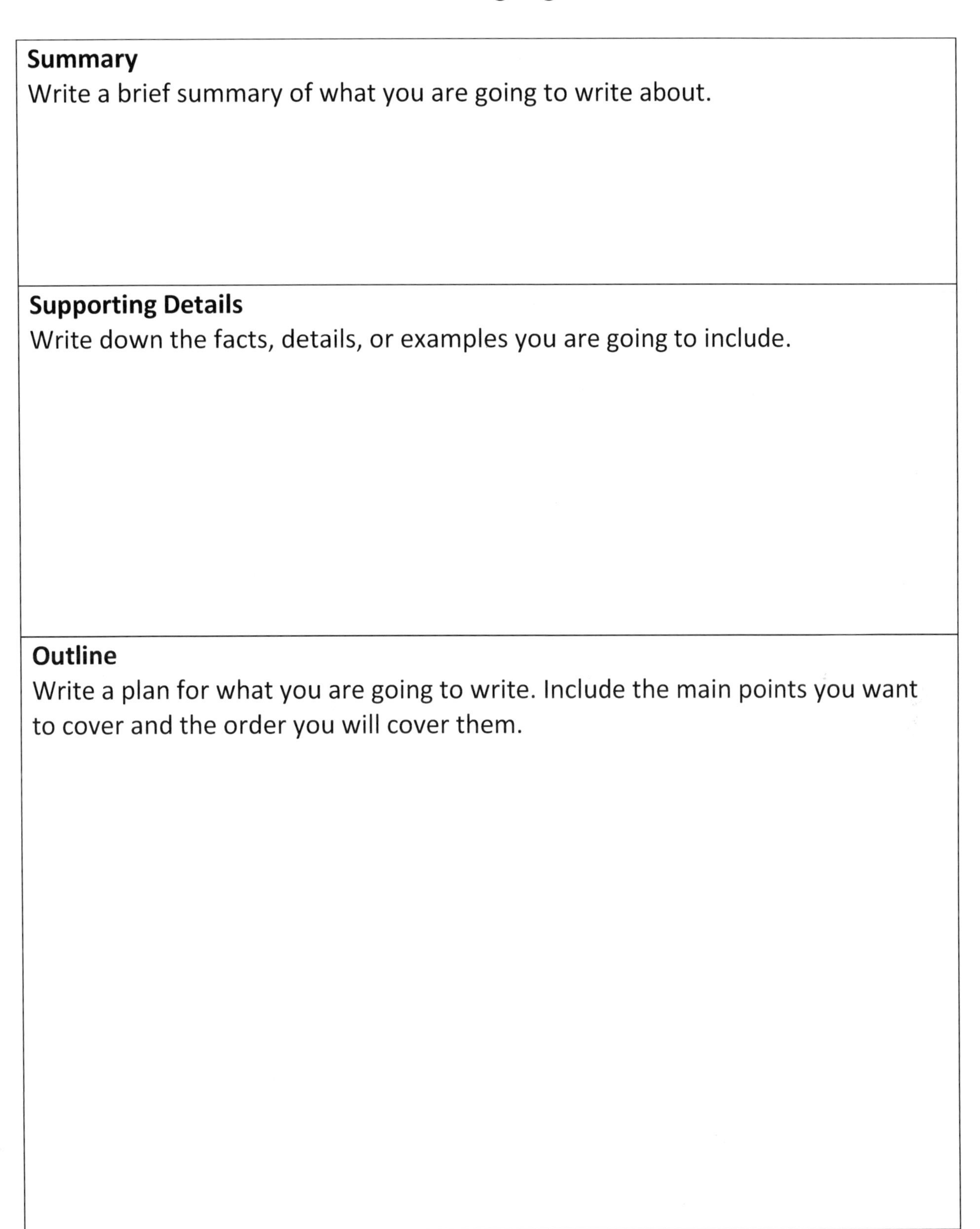

Summary

Write a brief summary of what you are going to write about.

Supporting Details

Write down the facts, details, or examples you are going to include.

Outline

Write a plan for what you are going to write. Include the main points you want to cover and the order you will cover them.

Task 4: Short Story Writing Task

Directions: Read the writing prompt below. Use the planning page to plan your writing. Then write or type your answer.

Joel was excited about moving into his new house. He really wanted to meet his new neighbors. He had seen kids about his age. They looked like they would be lots of fun.

Write a story about what happens when Joel meets his neighbors.

Hint

A good story has a beginning, middle, and end. As you plan your story, focus on what is going to happen in each part.

The beginning often introduces the characters, the setting, and the main problem. The start of this story might describe when Joel first meets his neighbors.

The middle of the story might describe what the neighbors are like, what happens when they meet, or something that goes wrong. This will be the main part of your story. It will usually be 2 or 3 paragraphs long. In this part, describe the events that take place.

At the end of the story, there is usually some sort of resolution. If something has gone wrong, it might be solved at this point. If Joel has learned something from his neighbors, this part might describe how he has changed. This ties up the story and makes it a complete story.

Planning Page

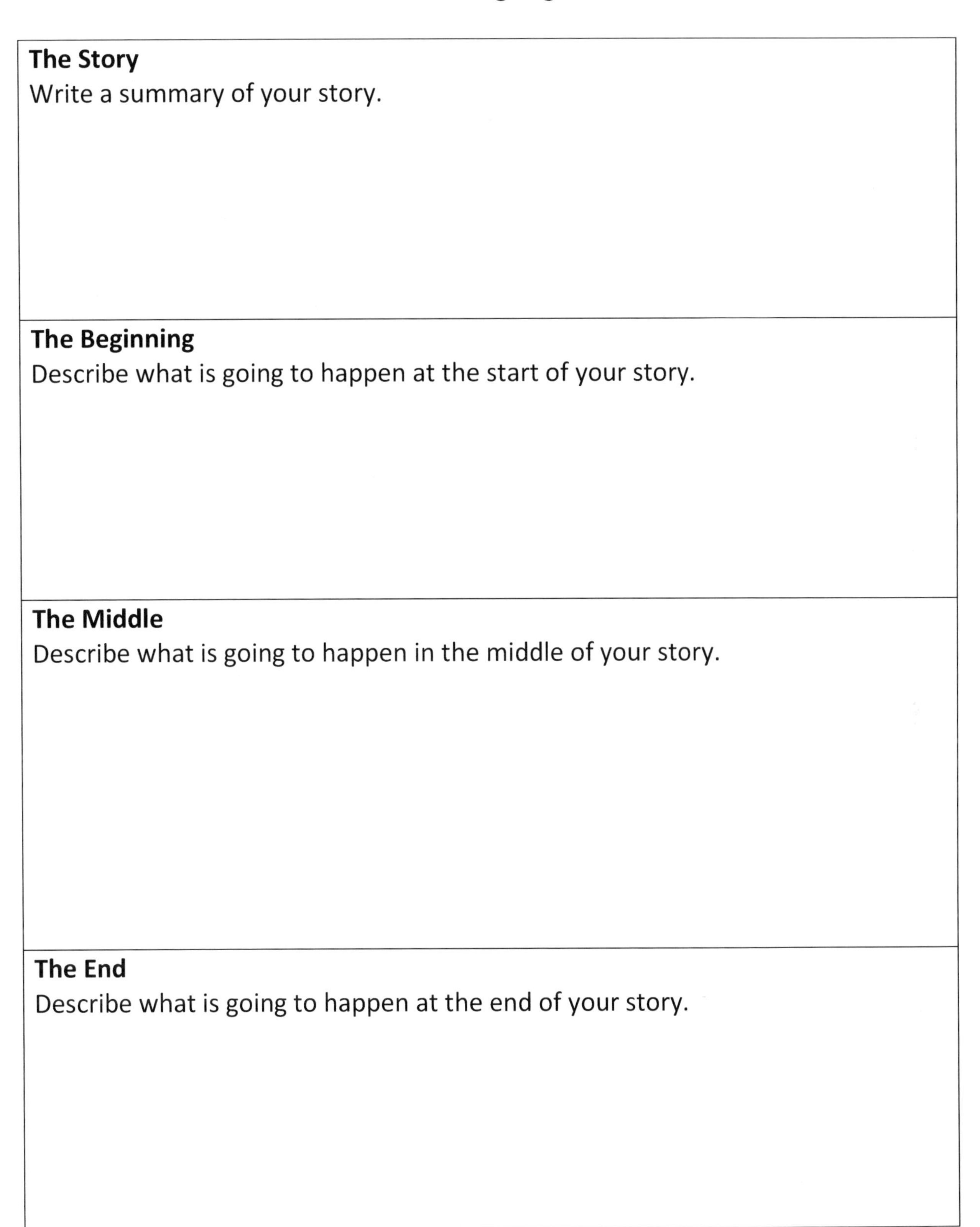

The Story

Write a summary of your story.

The Beginning

Describe what is going to happen at the start of your story.

The Middle

Describe what is going to happen in the middle of your story.

The End

Describe what is going to happen at the end of your story.

Writing and Editing Checklist

After you finish writing your story, you can use this guide to review and edit your work. Use the questions as a guide to finding ways you can improve your work.

Writing Checklist

- ✓ Does your story have a strong opening? Does it introduce the characters, the setting, or events well?
- ✓ Is your story well-organized? Do the events flow well?
- ✓ Does your story have an effective ending? Does it tie up the story well?
- ✓ Does your story include dialogue? If not, could dialogue make your story better?
- ✓ Have you used strong words? Are there words that could be replaced with better ones?
- ✓ Have you used effective descriptions? Could your descriptions be improved?
- ✓ Have you used sensory details? Could you add more sensory details to help readers imagine the scene?

Editing Checklist

- ✓ Have you used a variety of sentence structures? Are your sentences all written correctly?
- ✓ Is the grammar correct?
- ✓ Are all words spelled correctly? You can check the spelling of any words you are not sure of.
- ✓ Is punctuation used correctly?
- ✓ If dialogue is used, is it punctuated correctly?
- ✓ Are all words capitalized correctly?

Reading and Writing

Practice Set 5

This practice set contains four writing tasks. These are described below.

Task 1: Short Passage with Questions

This task has a short passage followed by questions. Read each question carefully. Then write your answer in the space provided.

You can also practice writing skills by completing the Core Skills Practice exercise.

Task 2: Short Passage with Questions

This task has a short passage followed by questions. Read each question carefully. Then write your answer in the space provided.

You can also practice writing skills by completing the Core Skills Practice exercise.

Task 3: Long Passage with Essay Question

This task has a longer passage with an essay question. Read the passage, complete the planning page, and then write or type your answer.

Task 4: Explanatory Writing Task

This final task requires you to write an essay that explains something. Read the writing prompt, complete the planning page, and then write or type your answer.

Task 1: Short Passage with Questions

The Olympics

The Olympics are a global sporting event. They feature both outdoor and indoor sports. They are watched and enjoyed by people all over the world. They are an important event because they bring people from all countries together.

They are held in both a summer and winter format. The Winter Olympics and Summer Olympics are both held every 4 years. The first modern Olympics were held in 1896. Many nations compete in each Olympic event. A different country hosts the games each time. The city of London in the United Kingdom was the host of the 2012 Olympics.

Year	Held
2012	London, United Kingdom
2008	Beijing, China
2004	Athens, Greece
2000	Sydney, Australia
1996	Atlanta, United States
1992	Barcelona, Spain

CORE SKILLS PRACTICE
WRITE A RESEARCH REPORT

Choose one Olympic athlete from the list below. Research and write a report on that athlete. Include what sport the athlete competed in, which Olympic Games he or she competed at, and the athlete's main achievements.

Michael Phelps
Carl Lewis
Muhammad Ali
Babe Didrickson
Mary Lou Retton

1 List **one** fact and **one** opinion given about the Olympics.

A fact is a statement that can be proven to be true. An opinion is a statement that cannot be proven to be true.

Fact: ____

____

Opinion: ____

____

2 Why do you think the Olympics is so popular all around the world?

This question is asking for your personal opinion. You can use details from the passage in your answer. You can also use your own knowledge and ideas.

____

____

____

____

____

____

Task 2: Short Passage with Questions

The Light

Christopher woke up late one evening. He was drawn to a light shining in through his window. It was not bright enough to be blinding, but it seemed to shimmer. Christopher almost felt like it was dancing. It seemed to pulse and slide from one color into another. He hurried downstairs and out into the back garden. Something bright and dazzling glimmered in the sky above him. It seemed to be shining a spotlight on his home.

Christopher shielded his eyes as the strange craft moved towards him. It finally rested before him on the grass. It gave him a sense of calm that made any fear he had disappear. It seemed happy and welcoming. As he stepped backwards, a door opened. A strange green outstretched arm welcomed him aboard. He paused, before stepping forward into the light.

CORE SKILLS PRACTICE

Imagine that Christopher wants to write a letter to a friend to tell what happened. Complete the summary of the events from Christopher's point of view. You can include what Christopher saw and how he felt.

I woke up late last night. You probably won't believe what I saw.

____

____

____

____

____

____

1 How does the author help the reader imagine the light?

Hint Focus on the words and phrases the author uses to describe the light. List these words and phrases in your answer and explain their impact.

____

____

____

____

____

____

2 Do you think Christopher feels curious or afraid at the end of the passage? Use details from the passage to support your answer.

____

____

____

____

____

____

3 What do you think the light is? What do you think happens next in the passage? Use details from the passage in your answer.

Hint

This question is asking you to draw a conclusion about what the light is. Use the details given in the passage to draw your conclusion. Then make a prediction about what happens to Christopher next.

Writing and Editing Checklist

After you finish writing your answer to question 3, you can use this guide to review and edit your work. Use the questions as a guide to finding ways you can improve your work.

Writing Checklist

- ✓ Have you clearly explained what the light is?
- ✓ Have you used details from the passage to explain how you decided what the light is?
- ✓ Have you included a prediction about what happens next?
- ✓ Does your prediction seem logical and make sense?
- ✓ Do your ideas flow well? Have you used words and phrases to link ideas well?

Editing Checklist

- ✓ Have you used a variety of sentence structures? Are your sentences all written correctly?
- ✓ Is the grammar correct?
- ✓ Are all words spelled correctly? You can check the spelling of any words you are not sure of.
- ✓ Is punctuation used correctly?
- ✓ Are all words capitalized correctly?

Task 3: Long Passage with Essay Question

Directions: Read the passage below. Then answer the question that follows. Use the planning page to plan your writing. Then write or type your essay.

Baseball

Baseball is a bat and ball sport that is very popular in America. It is a game played between two teams of nine players. The aim of the game is to score runs. Players strike the ball with a bat. Then they run around four bases. When they cross home base again, they have scored a run. Home base is also known as the home plate. The bases are set at each corner of a 90-foot square called the diamond.

Each team takes it in turns to bat while the other fields. The other team must stop the batters from scoring runs by getting them out. To get a batter out, they can strike them out. This means that the batter misses the ball three times. They can also get them out by catching the ball if the batter isn't safe on a base. Players can stop at any of the four bases once they have hit the ball, which makes them safe.

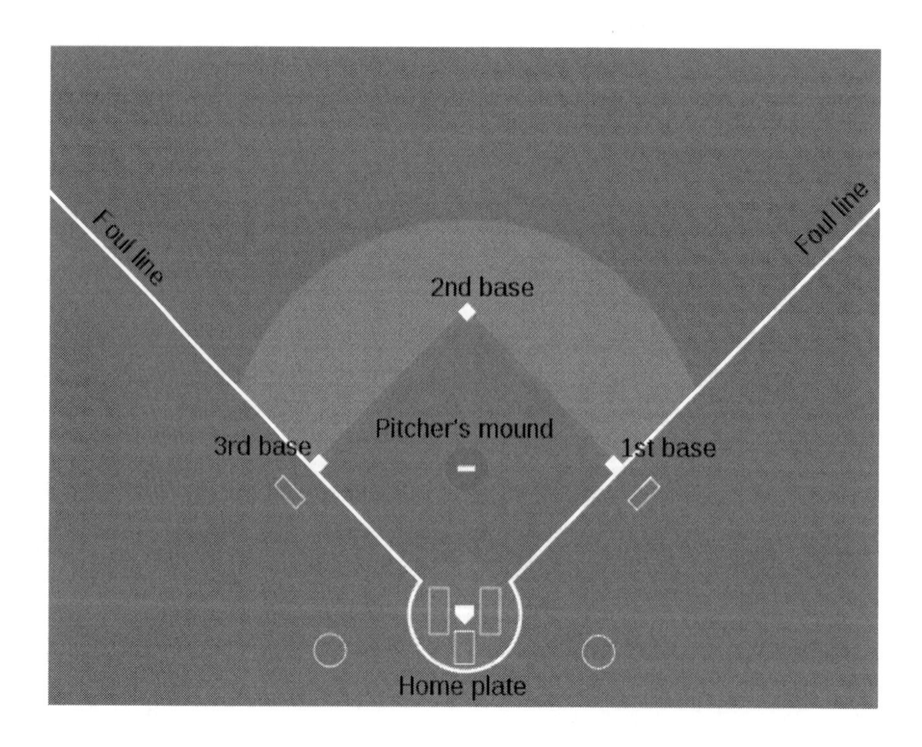

Once three players are out, the fielding team takes their turn to bat. Each time a team bats, it is known as an innings. There are nine innings in a professional league game. The team that scores the most runs at the close of all innings is the winner. The player who throws the ball to the batting team is known as the pitcher. Each professional game has at least two umpires who ensure fair play between the teams. Some big games have six umpires. There is one at each base and another two along the foul lines. The umpires know that their decisions could change the game, so they watch their areas closely.

The umpires judge whether players on the batting team are out or not. This usually means working out whether the player touched the base before the fielder touched the base with the ball. Umpires also decide whether or not pitchers throw the ball correctly. For example, a pitcher must have one foot on the pitcher's mound at the start of every pitch. The umpires also judge whether each pitch passes through the batter's strike zone. If the ball does pass through, the pitch will count as a strike even if the batter does not swing. If the ball is too high or too wide, it is counted as a ball.

The umpire watches closely. If the runner reaches the base before the fielder receives the ball, he will be safe and will not be out.

Baseball developed from the traditional bat and ball games of the 18th century. It has a sister sport referred to as rounders. Both of these sports were first played in America by British and Irish immigrants. It has since developed to become known as the national sport of North America. Over the last 20 years, the sport has also grown worldwide. It is now very popular in the Caribbean, South America, and many parts of Asia.

Baseball is a great sport for young kids. It is safer than contact sports like football. It requires a range of skills. Players can focus on being good batters, pitchers, or fielders. At the same time, players learn to work together as a team.

1 Think about what skills a good baseball player would need. Write an essay in which you describe the skills needed for a batter, a fielder, and a pitcher. Use details from the passage in your answer.

In your answer, be sure to
- describe the skills needed for a good batter
- describe the skills needed for a good fielder
- describe the skills needed for a good pitcher
- write an answer of between 1 and 2 pages

Hint

This essay question is asking you to use information from the passage to draw your own conclusions. The passage does not state the skills a good batter, fielder, or pitcher would need. However, it does describe what each of these players does and what the role involves. You have to use this information to decide what skills would be needed.

When you plan your work, list one or two main skills needed for each role. Then write your essay with a paragraph describing the skills needed for each role.

Planning Page

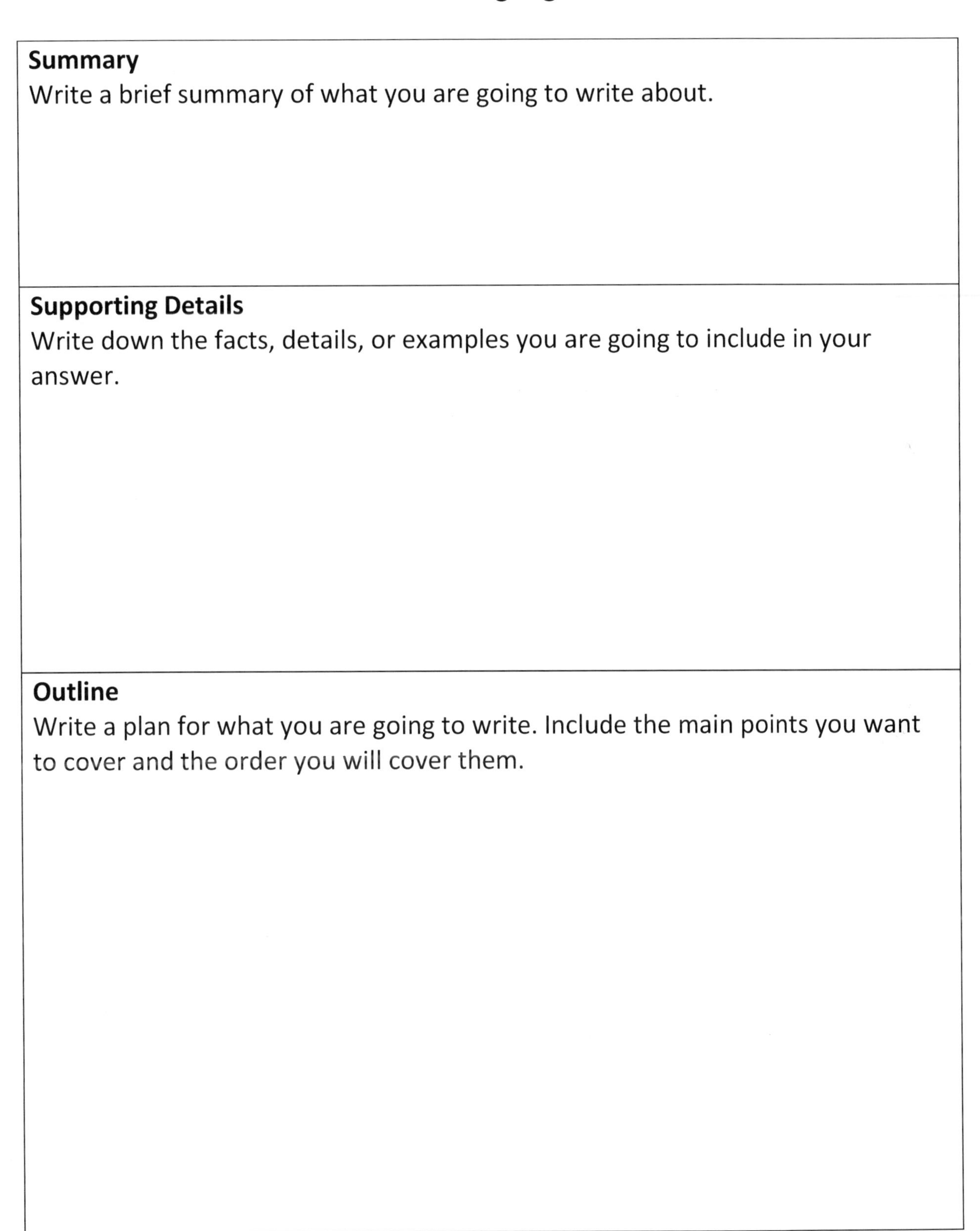

Summary
Write a brief summary of what you are going to write about.

Supporting Details
Write down the facts, details, or examples you are going to include in your answer.

Outline
Write a plan for what you are going to write. Include the main points you want to cover and the order you will cover them.

Task 4: Explanatory Writing Task

Directions: Read the writing prompt below. Use the planning page to plan your writing. Then write or type your answer.

Tiny Treasures

Tiny heart with a tiny beat,
Like the softness of a thousand tiny feet.
Smile that stretches far and wide,
My body feels warm and glows inside.
Just met my new baby sister today,
Now I wouldn't have life any other way.

The poet describes an important event for her family. Write a composition about an important event for your family. Describe the event and explain why it was an important event for your family.

This writing task introduces the topic by using a poem. You do not have to refer to the poem in your answer. The poem is just there to help you start thinking about the topic.

The goal of your writing is to write about an important event for your family. You should clearly describe the event and explain why it was important for your family. You could write about a positive event like a new baby being born like in the poem, or a difficult event such as when your family moved to a new town. Whatever event you choose, include examples and details to show why the event was important. You might describe how you felt, how the event changed your family, or what problems the event caused.

Planning Page

Summary

Write a brief summary of what you are going to write about.

Outline

Write a plan for what you are going to write. Include the main points you want to cover and the order you will cover them.

Writing and Editing Checklist

After you finish writing your essay, you can use this guide to review and edit your work. Use the questions as a guide to finding ways you can improve your work.

Writing Checklist

- ✓ Does your work have a strong opening? Does it introduce the topic and the main ideas?
- ✓ Is your work well-organized? Is related information grouped together? Does each paragraph have one main idea?
- ✓ Have you included facts, details, and examples to support your ideas?
- ✓ Is your work focused? Are there any details that do not fit with your main ideas?
- ✓ Do your ideas flow well? Have you used words and phrases to link ideas well?
- ✓ Does your work have a strong ending?

Editing Checklist

- ✓ Have you used a variety of sentence structures? Are your sentences all written correctly?
- ✓ Is the grammar correct?
- ✓ Are all words spelled correctly? You can check the spelling of any words you are not sure of.
- ✓ Is punctuation used correctly?
- ✓ Are all words capitalized correctly?

Reading and Writing

Practice Set 6

This practice set contains four writing tasks. These are described below.

Task 1: Short Passage with Questions

This task has a short passage followed by questions. Read each question carefully. Then write your answer in the space provided.

You can also practice writing skills by completing the Core Skills Practice exercise.

Task 2: Short Passage with Questions

This task has a short passage followed by questions. Read each question carefully. Then write your answer in the space provided.

You can also practice writing skills by completing the Core Skills Practice exercise.

Task 3: Short Story Writing Task

This task requires you to write a short story. Read the writing prompt, complete the planning page, and then write or type your answer.

Task 4: Opinion Piece Writing Task

This final task requires you to write an opinion piece. Read the writing prompt, complete the planning page, and then write or type your answer.

Task 1: Short Passage with Questions

Peace and Not War

Terry was watching football in the lounge room, when his younger brother Mark walked in and changed the channel. Mark was determined to watch his favorite cartoon. They fought over the remote control. Then they started arguing.

"I hate watching football," Mark yelled.

"I hate watching cartoons," Terry yelled back.

Their voices got louder and louder. The lounge room began to sound like a zoo. Their mother came in from the kitchen. Without saying anything, she picked up the remote and turned off the television.

"If you can't watch the television nicely, then you can't watch it at all," she said.

CORE SKILLS PRACTICE

Think of an argument you have had with someone. Describe who you argued with and what you argued about.

____

____

____

____

____

____

____

1 Why do Mark and Terry fight? Use details from the passage in your answer.

Hint To answer this question, do not just write that they fight over the television. Explain why they fight over the television.

2 The author says that the lounge room "began to sound like a zoo." Explain what the author means by this.

Task 2: Short Passage with Questions

The Dodo

The dodo was a species of flightless bird that became extinct. It lived on the island of Mauritius. It lived in an environment free from ground-based predators. When humans arrived on the island, they brought with them many ground-based animals. These included rats, pigs, and dogs. These animals ate dodo's eggs from their nests. The eggs were easy to get to because the nests were on the ground. Humans also hunted dodos for their meat. Humans also destroyed the dodo's forest habitats. The number of dodos decreased until they became extinct.

The dodo will always be remembered because it led to a common phrase. The slang phrase "as dead as a dodo" is used to describe something that is gone forever or definitely dead.

CORE SKILLS PRACTICE
WRITE A RESEARCH REPORT

The dodo is one animal that has become extinct, but it is not the only one. Choose one extinct animal from the list below. Use the Internet to find out why the animal became extinct. Then write a report describing your findings.

mammoth
mastodon
megalodon
saber-toothed cat
Tasmanian tiger

1 Explain what common phrase refers to the dodo and describe what the phrase means.

Hint This question is asking you to summarize specific information given in the passage. Make sure you use your own words when writing your answer.

____

____

____

____

____

____

2 Give **three** reasons that dodos became extinct.

1: ____

____

2: ____

____

3: ____

____

Task 3: Short Story Writing Task

Directions: Read the writing prompt below. Use the planning page to plan your writing. Then write or type your answer.

Look at the picture below.

Write a story based on what is happening in the picture.

Hint

You should use the picture to come up with an idea for your story. The picture shows two people trying to start a fire. Think about why they might be doing this. Are they lost in the woods and it is getting dark? Are they camping and have forgotten to bring a camping stove to heat their food?

A good story will often be based around a main problem that a character overcomes. Focus on thinking of what the character's main problem is, and develop a complete story based on solving this problem.

Planning Page

The Story
Write a summary of your story.

The Beginning
Describe what is going to happen at the start of your story.

The Middle
Describe what is going to happen in the middle of your story.

The End
Describe what is going to happen at the end of your story.

Task 4: Opinion Piece Writing Task

Directions: Read the writing prompt below. Use the planning page to plan your writing. Then write or type your answer.

Your school has decided that it wants a new mascot. Think of an animal that you think would make a good mascot.

Write an essay for your school newspaper. In the essay, you should persuade people to agree that the animal you have selected would make a good mascot. Use reasons, facts, or details in your essay.

Hint

The key to writing a good essay is to support it well! It does not matter what animal you choose. However, you should come up with reasons to support your choice. Make sure you describe these reasons in your essay.

You might describe why the animal would suit your school. For example, it might be an animal that lives in the area. You might also describe the qualities of the animal. For example, you might choose bees because they work well as part of a team or dolphins because they are intelligent. Once you have chosen your animal, decide on two or three reasons you can use in your essay. Focus on making strong arguments based on your reasons.

Planning Page

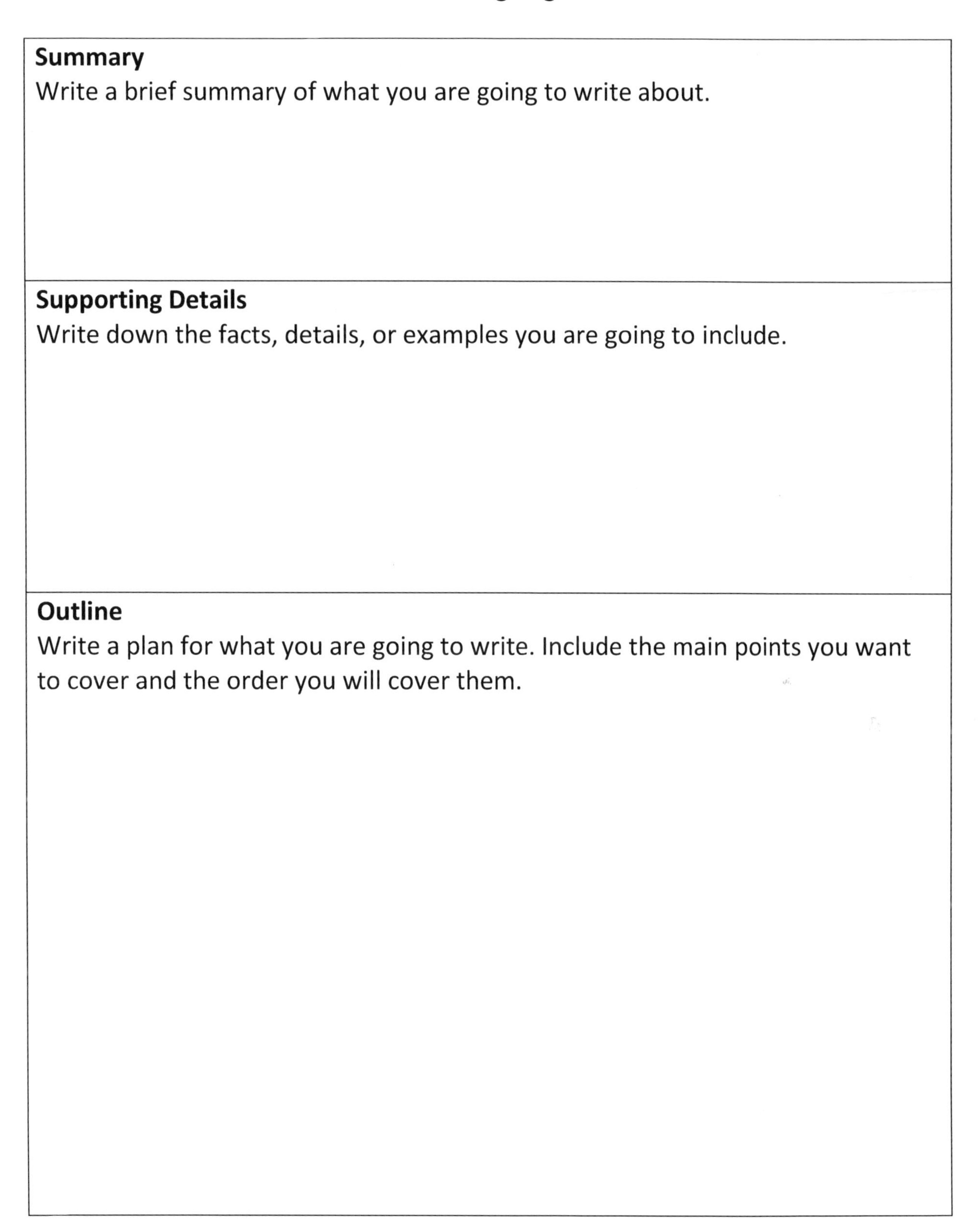
Summary
Write a brief summary of what you are going to write about.

Supporting Details
Write down the facts, details, or examples you are going to include.

Outline
Write a plan for what you are going to write. Include the main points you want to cover and the order you will cover them.

Writing and Editing Checklist

After you finish writing your opinion piece, you can use this guide to review and edit your work. Use the questions as a guide to finding ways you can improve your work.

Writing Checklist

- ✓ Does your work have one clear opinion?
- ✓ Does your work have a strong opening? Does the opening introduce the topic and state the opinion?
- ✓ Is your opinion supported? Have you used facts, details, and examples to support your opinion?
- ✓ Is your work well-organized? Is related information grouped together? Does each paragraph have one main idea?
- ✓ Do your ideas flow well? Have you used words and phrases to link ideas well?
- ✓ Does your work have a strong ending? Does the ending restate the main idea and tie up the opinion piece?

Editing Checklist

- ✓ Have you used a variety of sentence structures? Are your sentences all written correctly?
- ✓ Is the grammar correct?
- ✓ Are all words spelled correctly? You can check the spelling of any words you are not sure of.
- ✓ Is punctuation used correctly?
- ✓ Are all words capitalized correctly?

Reading and Writing

Practice Set 7

This practice set contains four writing tasks. These are described below.

Task 1: Short Passage with Questions

This task has a short passage followed by questions. Read each question carefully. Then write your answer in the space provided.

You can also practice writing skills by completing the Core Skills Practice exercise.

Task 2: Short Passage with Questions

This task has a short passage followed by questions. Read each question carefully. Then write your answer in the space provided.

You can also practice writing skills by completing the Core Skills Practice exercise.

Task 3: Long Passage with Essay Question

This task has a longer passage with an essay question. Read the passage, complete the planning page, and then write or type your answer.

Task 4: Personal Narrative Writing Task

This final task requires you to write a personal narrative. Read the writing prompt, complete the planning page, and then write or type your answer.

Task 1: Short Passage with Questions

Letter to the Editor

Dear Editor,

I am worried that our town park does not look as nice as it once did. It is not as well-cared for and is not cleaned as often. There are food wrappers, cans, and even broken glass lying around. I've noticed that there is a lot of graffiti appearing too.

I think that something must be done about this! It is no longer a lovely place to spend time. It is not even a safe place to play with all the trash lying around. The people of our town need to demand that something be done about this.

Yours with hope,

Evan

CORE SKILLS PRACTICE

Think about the problem that Evan is describing. How do you think the problem could be solved? Write a paragraph describing your solution to the problem.

____

____

____

____

____

____

1 Complete the web below using information from the article.

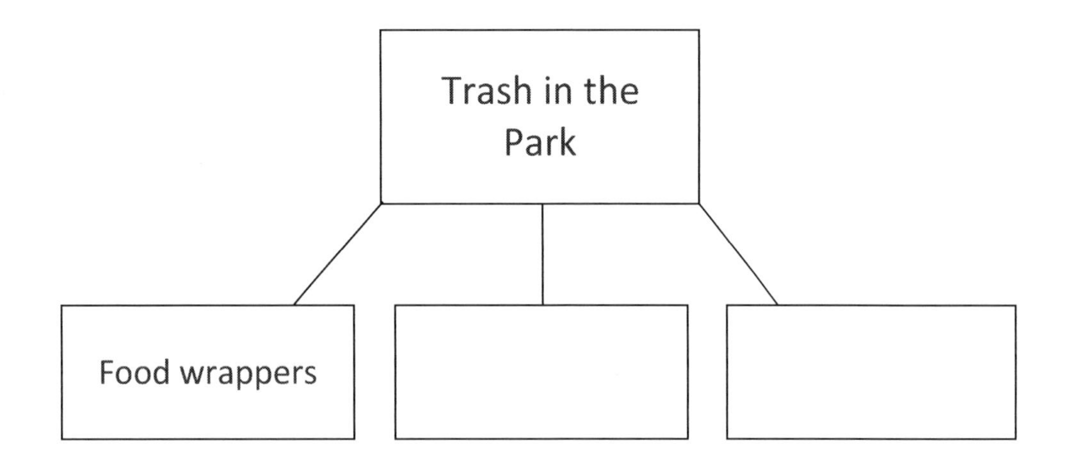

2 Evan argues that the town park does not look as nice as it once did. How do you think Evan could make this argument more convincing?

Hint Think about what information Evan could include to help readers better understand what the park looks like now, or how the park has changed.

____

____

____

____

____

____

Task 2: Short Passage with Questions

Tom's Time Machine

Tom had spent almost a decade designing and building his time machine. He had spent countless hours in his laboratory. After he developed it, he had done many experiments sending small objects through time. And now, after all his hard work, it was finally time to test it for himself. He entered the time machine, and began to type into the computer.

Tom had always wanted to go back to the dinosaur age. He set the time to 80 million years ago. As the machine went dark and began to shake, he knew he was on his way deep into the unknown. He was scared, but thrilled with the idea that he might see a real dinosaur. He just hoped to himself that the first one he saw was friendly.

CORE SKILLS PRACTICE
WRITE A SHORT STORY

If you had a time machine, what time would you travel to? It could be a time far in the past like Tom, a time more recently in the past, or a time in the future. Imagine you have traveled to that time. Write a story describing your journey. Answer the questions below to help plan your story. Then write your story.

What time would you travel to?

____

What would you do once you arrived?

____

What would the past or future look like?

____

1 Circle the word below that best describes Tom. Then explain why you chose that word.

adventurous **brave** **determined**

____

____

____

____

____

2 What genre is the passage? Explain how you can tell.

Hint

Genre refers to the category a work of literature falls into. Common genres include mystery, fantasy, horror, adventure, science fiction, and historical fiction.

____

____

____

____

____

____

Task 3: Long Passage with Essay Question

Directions: Read the passage below. Then answer the question that follows. Use the planning page to plan your writing. Then write or type your essay.

July 25, 2014

Dear Uncle Yuri,

Today was quite an amazing day for me. It was the day that my father returned home from overseas. He had been away from us for over a year.

He was chosen to work on a special research project in London. He and his team were working on a new way to make recycled paper products. It would use less water and energy and be better for the environment. Although we were proud of him, we longed for the day when he would wake up under the same roof as us. We had missed him more than words could ever say. Now the day had finally arrived. He had worked hard and it was time for him to return home.

Mom woke us at 6 a.m. to head to the airport. My father's flight was due in at 9:30.

"We don't want to be late!" she kept saying as she woke everyone up.

She had no need to remind me! I quickly dressed, washed, and made my way downstairs for breakfast. I could not take my eyes off the clock all morning. Time was going so slowly. When the clock struck 8:45, my mom told us all it was time to go. We all raced to the car and made our way quickly to the airport.

We arrived just after 9 and hurried to the terminal to wait. But 9:30 came and went and our father's flight had still not arrived. Another 10 minutes went by, and I started pacing up and down. I kept asking Mom where he was. She just kept smiling and saying he'd be there soon. I searched the crowds of people, hoping to see his familiar face. I stood as tall as I could to try and see every person coming through the gate.

Then suddenly a gap appeared in the crowd and a tall shadow emerged. There was my father standing before me. He dropped his bags to the floor and swept my sister and I up in his arms.

"I've missed you so much," he said through tears of joy.

We all cried together. I never want my father to ever let me go.

Today was pretty perfect.

Holly

1 How can you tell that Holly is excited about seeing her father? Use details from the passage to support your answer.

In your answer, be sure to
- describe how you can tell that Holly is excited about seeing her father
- use details from the passage in your answer
- write an answer of between 1 and 2 pages

Hint

The question asks you to find details that support an idea. The question tells you that Holly is excited about seeing her father. Read the passage and look for details and examples that show that she is excited. This could be what she says. It could also be how she acts, such as the way she keeps looking at the clock. Choose three or four details and use these in your answer.

Planning Page

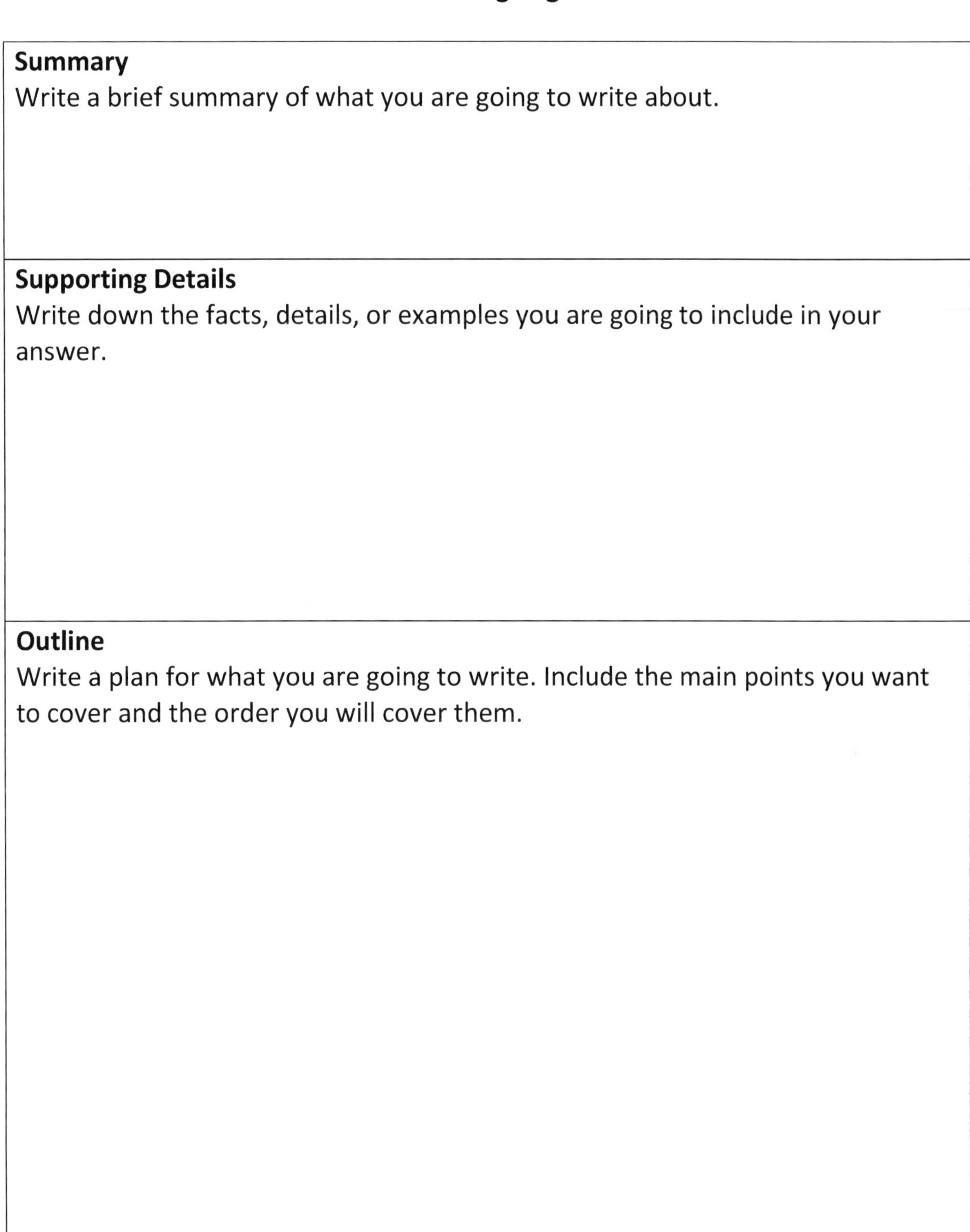

Summary

Write a brief summary of what you are going to write about.

Supporting Details

Write down the facts, details, or examples you are going to include in your answer.

Outline

Write a plan for what you are going to write. Include the main points you want to cover and the order you will cover them.

Task 4: Personal Narrative Writing Task

Directions: Read the writing prompt below. Use the planning page to plan your writing. Then write or type your answer.

Good friends and family members can sometimes have misunderstandings. Think about a time when you had a misunderstanding with a friend or family member.

Write a composition describing a misunderstanding that you had with a friend or family member. Describe what the misunderstanding was, what happened because of the misunderstanding, and what you think of the misunderstanding now.

Hint

When planning your writing, it is a good idea to break down what you want to say into paragraphs. This will help make sure your writing is well-organized and easy to understand. In your outline, describe what you are going to cover in each paragraph. For example, your outline could be something like this:

Introduction - what the misunderstanding was
Paragraph 1 - how the misunderstanding caused a fight
Paragraph 2 - how I realized that I was wrong
Paragraph 3 - how I fixed things by saying sorry
Conclusion - how I learned to listen to others and not always think that I am right

Planning Page

Summary

Write a brief summary of what you are going to write about.

Outline

Write a plan for what you are going to write. Include the main points you want to cover and the order you will cover them.

Writing and Editing Checklist

After you finish writing your personal narrative, you can use this guide to review and edit your work. Use the questions as a guide to finding ways you can improve your work.

Writing Checklist

- ✓ Does your work have a strong opening? Does it introduce the main ideas or set the scene well?
- ✓ Is your work well-organized? Is related information grouped together? Does each paragraph have one main idea?
- ✓ Does your work have an effective ending? Does it tie up the events well?
- ✓ Is your work focused? Are there any details that do not fit with your main ideas?
- ✓ Do your ideas flow well? Have you used words and phrases to link ideas well?
- ✓ Have you used strong words? Are there words that could be replaced with better ones?
- ✓ Have you used effective descriptions? Could your descriptions be improved?
- ✓ Have you used sensory details? Could you add more sensory details to help readers imagine the scene?

Editing Checklist

- ✓ Have you used a variety of sentence structures? Are your sentences all written correctly?
- ✓ Is the grammar correct?
- ✓ Are all words spelled correctly? You can check the spelling of any words you are not sure of.
- ✓ Is punctuation used correctly?
- ✓ If dialogue is used, is it punctuated correctly?
- ✓ Are all words capitalized correctly?

Reading and Writing

Practice Set 8

This practice set contains four writing tasks. These are described below.

Task 1: Short Passage with Questions

This task has a short passage followed by questions. Read each question carefully. Then write your answer in the space provided.

You can also practice writing skills by completing the Core Skills Practice exercise.

Task 2: Short Passage with Questions

This task has a short passage followed by questions. Read each question carefully. Then write your answer in the space provided.

You can also practice writing skills by completing the Core Skills Practice exercise.

Task 3: Opinion Piece Writing Task

This task requires you to write an opinion piece. Read the writing prompt, complete the planning page, and then write or type your answer.

Task 4: Short Story Writing Task

This task requires you to write a short story. Read the writing prompt, complete the planning page, and then write or type your answer.

Task 1: Short Passage with Questions

Sugar

Did you know that sugar is a type of crystal? The crystal is edible. It is made out of a fructose molecule and a glucose molecule bonded together to form tiny crystals. It can form large crystals or fine crystals. Large crystals can be crushed or ground down to make finer crystals.

When heated, sugar crystals will begin to melt. They change from solid white particles to a thick liquid. As they are cooked further, they take on a brown color and a nutty flavor develops. This process is called caramelization. This process is often used to make sweets such as toffees and syrups.

Crunchy Toffee

1. Place 1 cup of sugar and ¼ cup of water in a saucepan.
2. Stir as the mixture is heating until all of the sugar has dissolved.
3. Bring the mixture to the boil and continue boiling until the mixture is a dark golden color.
4. Pour the mixture onto a baking tray and allow to cool.
5. Once it is cool, break the toffee into shards.

This crispy toffee is perfect with desserts, on ice cream, or you can even add peanuts to it when it is cooling to make a crunchy peanut toffee.

CORE SKILLS PRACTICE
WRITE A RECIPE

Sugar is used to make many things. The list below describes some common desserts that are made using sugar. Choose one of the desserts and research how it is made. Then write your own recipe describing how to make it.

caramel apples meringue candied almonds peanut brittle

1 Describe **two** things you learned about sugar.

Use the inforrmation in the passage to answer this question. But make sure you write your answer in your own words.

1: ____

____

2: ____

____

2 What would you do if you wanted sugar to undergo caramelization?

____

____

____

____

____

____

Task 2: Short Passage with Questions

Creature Comforts

Fred the farmer loved his job. He enjoyed nothing more than waking up at sunrise to feed and tend to his animals. He would even sing to them as he visited them in the morning. Even during the cold days of winter, he never once complained. He just put on thick socks and an extra coat and went out into the freezing cold air. The wind whipped around him and tried to annoy him. But Fred just focused on his tasks.

When the summer sun rose high in the sky and the day became hot, he still loved working hard. He was always pleased knowing that he was making his animals happy and comfortable. Although they couldn't speak, Fred knew that his animals were happy with their life on his farm.

CORE SKILLS PRACTICE

The passage describes how Fred loves being a farmer. Do you think you would enjoy being a farmer? Explain why or why not.

____

____

____

____

____

____

____

1 What is the main theme of the passage?

Hint

The theme of a passage is the idea it expresses, or a lesson it aims to teach.

2 Identify the personification used in the first paragraph. Then explain why the author used it.

Hint

Personification is a literary technique where objects are given human qualities, or described as if they are human.

3 What do you think matters most to Fred? Use details from the passage to support your answer.

Hint Start by stating what you think matters most to Fred. Then explain why you think this. Use two or three details from the passage to support your answer.

Writing and Editing Checklist

After you finish writing your answer to question 3, you can use this guide to review and edit your work. Use the questions as a guide to finding ways you can improve your work.

Writing Checklist

- ✓ Does your work have a strong opening? Does it introduce the topic and the main ideas?
- ✓ Is your work well-organized? Is related information grouped together? Does each paragraph have one main idea?
- ✓ Have you clearly explained what matters most to Fred? Have you used details from the passage to support your claims?
- ✓ Is your work focused? Are there any details that do not fit with your main ideas?
- ✓ Do your ideas flow well? Have you used words and phrases to link ideas well?

Editing Checklist

- ✓ Have you used a variety of sentence structures? Are your sentences all written correctly?
- ✓ Is the grammar correct?
- ✓ Are all words spelled correctly? You can check the spelling of any words you are not sure of.
- ✓ Is punctuation used correctly?
- ✓ Are all words capitalized correctly?

Task 3: Opinion Piece Writing Task

Directions: Read the writing prompt below. Use the planning page to plan your writing. Then write or type your answer.

Read this proverb about work.

Many hands make light work.

Do you agree with this proverb? Explain why or why not. Use facts, details, or examples in your answer.

Hint

A proverb is a short saying that states an idea. The idea in this proverb is that many people make work easier. You have to explain whether or not you agree with this. When you are asked whether or not you agree with something, you will not be scored based on whether you agree or not. You will be scored on how well you explain why you do or do not agree.

Don't worry about choosing the right answer. Instead, focus on what your personal opinion is. Then focus on clearly explaining why this is your opinion and giving reasons that will persuade other people to agree with you.

Planning Page

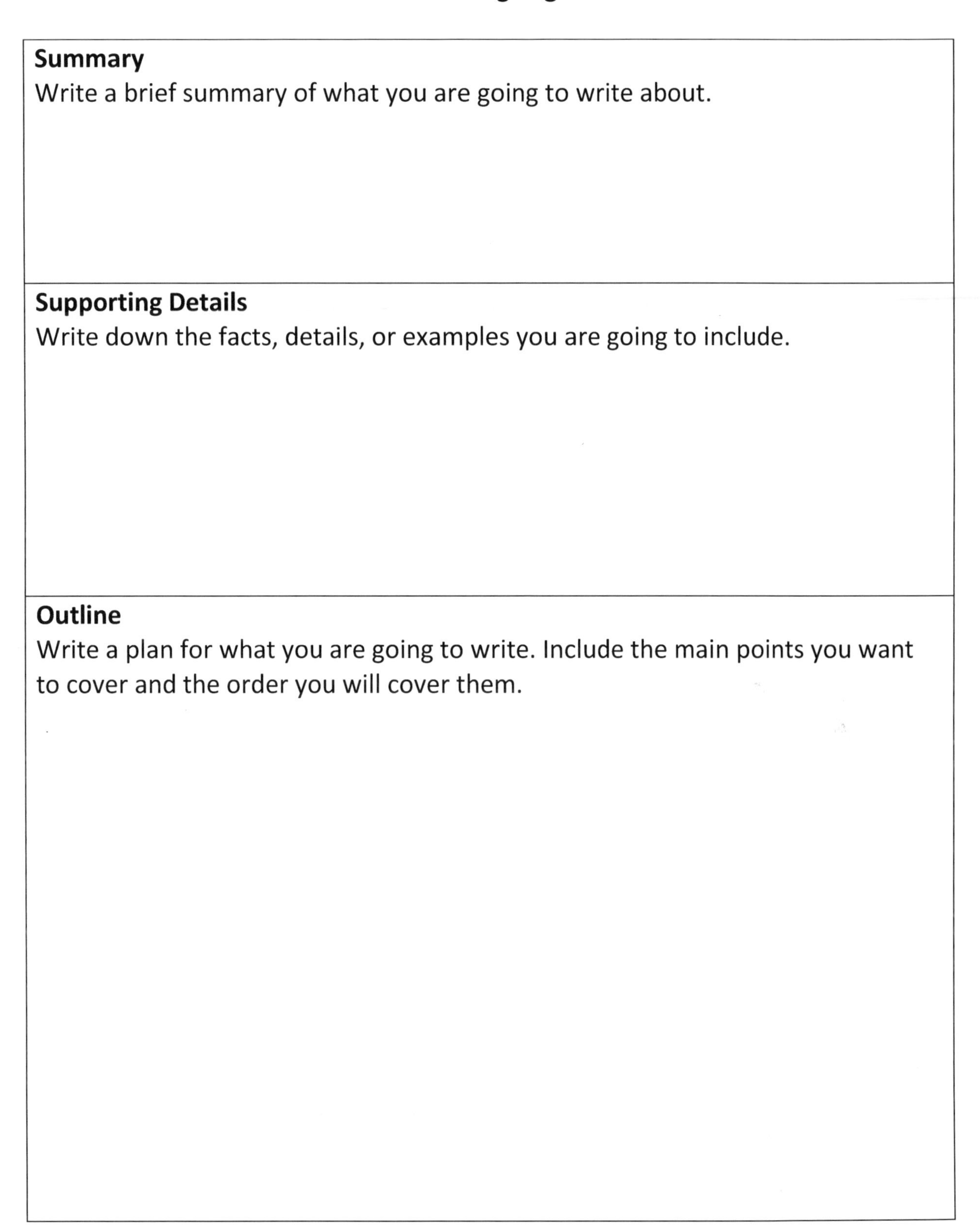

Summary

Write a brief summary of what you are going to write about.

Supporting Details

Write down the facts, details, or examples you are going to include.

Outline

Write a plan for what you are going to write. Include the main points you want to cover and the order you will cover them.

Task 4: Short Story Writing Task

Directions: Read the writing prompt below. Use the planning page to plan your writing. Then write or type your answer.

Look at the picture below.

Write a story based on what is happening in the picture.

The setting of your story does not have to be the present. The picture suggests that this story could be set long ago. Use your imagination to think of an interesting story that could take place in an earlier time. Try to make sure all the details fit with the setting. For example, if your story has dialogue, try and write it how you imagine people might have spoken long ago.

Planning Page

The Story
Write a summary of your story.

The Beginning
Describe what is going to happen at the start of your story.

The Middle
Describe what is going to happen in the middle of your story.

The End
Describe what is going to happen at the end of your story.

Writing and Editing Checklist

After you finish writing your story, you can use this guide to review and edit your work. Use the questions as a guide to finding ways you can improve your work.

Writing Checklist

- ✓ Does your story have a strong opening? Does it introduce the characters, the setting, or events well?
- ✓ Is your story well-organized? Do the events flow well?
- ✓ Does your story have an effective ending? Does it tie up the story well?
- ✓ Does your story include dialogue? If not, could dialogue make your story better?
- ✓ Have you used strong words? Are there words that could be replaced with better ones?
- ✓ Have you used effective descriptions? Could your descriptions be improved?
- ✓ Have you used sensory details? Could you add more sensory details to help readers imagine the scene?

Editing Checklist

- ✓ Have you used a variety of sentence structures? Are your sentences all written correctly?
- ✓ Is the grammar correct?
- ✓ Are all words spelled correctly? You can check the spelling of any words you are not sure of.
- ✓ Is punctuation used correctly?
- ✓ If dialogue is used, is it punctuated correctly?
- ✓ Are all words capitalized correctly?

Reading and Writing

Practice Set 9

This practice set contains four writing tasks. These are described below.

Task 1: Short Passage with Questions

This task has a short passage followed by questions. Read each question carefully. Then write your answer in the space provided.

You can also practice writing skills by completing the Core Skills Practice exercise.

Task 2: Short Passage with Questions

This task has a short passage followed by questions. Read each question carefully. Then write your answer in the space provided.

You can also practice writing skills by completing the Core Skills Practice exercise.

Task 3: Long Passage with Essay Question

This task has a longer passage with an essay question. Read the passage, complete the planning page, and then write or type your answer.

Task 4: Explanatory Writing Task

This final task requires you to write an essay that explains something. Read the writing prompt, complete the planning page, and then write or type your answer.

Task 1: Short Passage with Questions

Herbal Tea

1. Add water to a kettle and wait until it has boiled.
2. Rinse the cup with boiling water to warm it up.
3. Place a tea bag and a teaspoon or two of sugar (if required) in the cup.
4. Add the water and allow to sit for 30 seconds. You can let it sit for longer if you like your tea stronger.
5. Use a spoon to squeeze the tea bag. Then remove and stir the liquid.
6. If you like, you can also add a dash of milk or cream.

If you are making tea for several people, follow the same steps but use a teapot instead of a cup.

CORE SKILLS PRACTICE

There are different types of herbal teas. Research the benefits of different types of teas. Use the information to complete the table below.

Type of Tea	Main Benefit
Green tea	Lowers cholesterol
Peppermint tea	
Chamomile tea	

1 What is the main purpose of the passage?

Hint

When answering questions like this, you should state the general purpose of the passage. You should also support your answer by explaining how you can tell what the purpose is.

2 Describe **three** actions in the process of making tea that are optional.

1:

2:

3:

Task 2: Short Passage with Questions

A Day in the Life

Jenny was so proud of her father. He was a local police officer. Jenny's father took great pride in protecting people and keeping them safe. Jenny loved it when her father came home in the evening. He would talk about everything that happened that day.

Sometimes he would tell how he tracked down a thief. Other times, he would describe how he directed traffic after an accident. Another day, he might tell how he pulled over people who were speeding. Some days, all he did was sit at his desk and do paperwork.

No matter what he told her, Jenny was always impressed. When she slept at night, Jenny would dream that one day she would be like her father.

CORE SKILLS PRACTICE
WRITE A SHORT STORY

Imagine that something exciting happens to Jenny's father the next time he goes to work. Write a short story describing the event. Answer the questions below to help plan your story. Then write your story.

What exciting event happens to Jenny's father?

____

What does Jenny's father do?

____

What happens in the end?

____

1 Complete the web below using information from the passage.

The center of the web tells you what the web is listing. Make sure you only complete the web with details that are included in the passage.

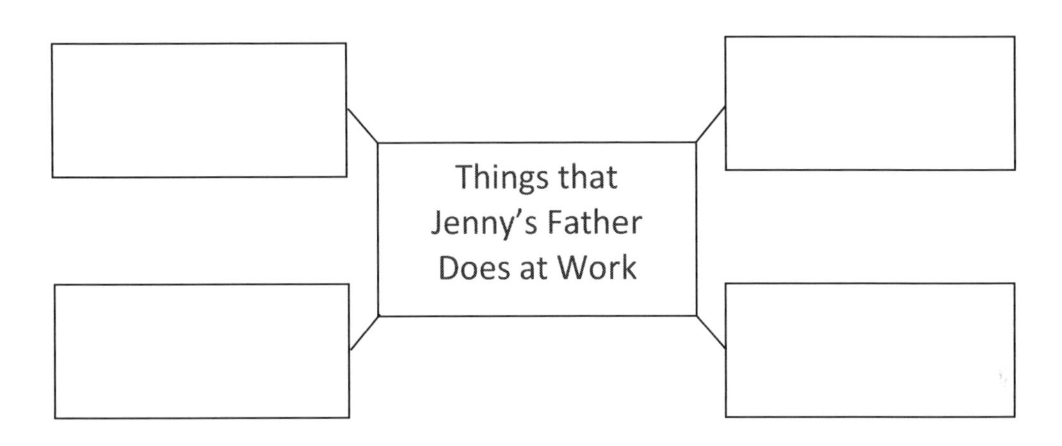

2 Explain why "A Day in the Life" is a suitable title for the passage.

____

____

____

____

____

____

Task 3: Long Passage with Essay Question

Directions: Read the passage below. Then answer the question that follows. Use the planning page to plan your writing. Then write or type your essay.

One Game for Two

Thomas could be quite mean at times. He had a younger brother called Simon and he rarely shared his toys with him.

"You must share Thomas," urged his mother. "One day you will want somebody to share something with you and they won't. Then you will be very upset."

Thomas just laughed his mother's advice off.

"I'll be fine," he replied. "As long as I have my own toys, I will always be fine."

His mother just shrugged her shoulders.

"Very well," she said. "It seems that you know best."

One day she decided to teach him a lesson. Both boys had been begging for a video game system for over a year. She decided that it was finally time to buy the boys the video game system and a few games.

When Christmas day arrived, both boys were patiently waiting for their presents in front of the fireplace. As Thomas tore into the video game package, his eyes lit up. It was the exact video game system he had wanted for so long.

Simon took longer than Thomas to carefully unwrap his own present. When he did, he was delighted to see three video games. He thanked his mother for not just getting him one great game, but getting him three.

Thomas raced over to check out the games. He saw they were the games he wanted as well and grinned.

"There is just one thing, Simon," Simon's mother said. "You don't have a system to play them on, so you're going to have to ask if you can use your brother's."

"But it's my present," Thomas said gruffly. "I don't want him to use it."

"I think you should be kinder and let your brother use it," his mother suggested.

"Do I have to?" Thomas whined.

"You don't have to," his mother said. "But it would be the right thing to do."

Thomas just shrugged. Then he shook his head.

"No," he said firmly. "I've wanted it for ages and I don't want him to break it."

Simon looked at his brother sadly. He wasn't surprised by his decision, but he was still upset by it.

"Very well," the mother said. "But I hope you realize you won't have much fun with your video game system without any games to play."

Thomas suddenly realized that Simon had games, but he didn't. Simon started to say that Thomas could play his games, but his mother stopped him.

“Since you don't want to share your system with Simon, it wouldn’t be fair for you to play his games,” the mother continued.

Now Thomas realized that he had a problem. He had the system, Simon had the games, and they needed both to be able to play.

Thomas paused and thought for a moment.

“Okay, I suppose I could share my video game system,” he whispered quietly. “That does seem fair.”

Simon quickly agreed to share his games and they spent the rest of the day playing a racing game together.

1 What do you think is the main message of the passage? How could you use this message in your own life? Use details from the passage in your answer.

In your answer, be sure to
- describe the main message of the passage
- relate the main message to your own life
- use details from the passage in your answer
- write an answer of between 1 and 2 pages

There are two parts to this writing task. You should start by describing what the message of the passage is. This is the lesson that Thomas learns, and also the lesson that readers learn. After describing the message, you should write about how it relates to you. Write a paragraph or two describing how you could use the message to help you in your own life.

Planning Page

Summary

Write a brief summary of what you are going to write about.

Supporting Details

Write down the facts, details, or examples you are going to include in your answer.

Outline

Write a plan for what you are going to write. Include the main points you want to cover and the order you will cover them.

Task 4: Explanatory Writing Task

Directions: Read the writing prompt below. Use the planning page to plan your writing. Then write or type your answer.

Do you share a room or do you have your own room? If you share a room, explain what the good and bad things are about sharing your room. If you have your own room, explain what the good and bad things are about having your own room.

Write an essay describing whether or not you share a room and explaining what you like and dislike about it.

Hint

When writing essays like this, you should focus on organizing your work well. The first paragraph should introduce the topic and explain whether or not you share a room. If you share a room, you could also include details about who you share a room with.

The writing prompt tells you to write about what you like about it and what you dislike about it. Start by writing a paragraph or two that tells what you like. Clearly state what you like and include details and examples to support your ideas. Then write a paragraph or two describing what you dislike. Again, use details and examples to support your ideas.

Finish the essay with a paragraph that sums up your main ideas.

Planning Page

Summary

Write a brief summary of what you are going to write about.

Outline

Write a plan for what you are going to write. Include the main points you want to cover and the order you will cover them.

Writing and Editing Checklist

After you finish writing your essay, you can use this guide to review and edit your work. Use the questions as a guide to finding ways you can improve your work.

Writing Checklist

- ✓ Does your work have a strong opening? Does it introduce the topic and the main ideas?
- ✓ Is your work well-organized? Is related information grouped together? Does each paragraph have one main idea?
- ✓ Have you included facts, details, and examples to support your ideas?
- ✓ Is your work focused? Are there any details that do not fit with your main ideas?
- ✓ Do your ideas flow well? Have you used words and phrases to link ideas well?
- ✓ Does your work have a strong ending?

Editing Checklist

- ✓ Have you used a variety of sentence structures? Are your sentences all written correctly?
- ✓ Is the grammar correct?
- ✓ Are all words spelled correctly? You can check the spelling of any words you are not sure of.
- ✓ Is punctuation used correctly?
- ✓ Are all words capitalized correctly?

Reading and Writing

Practice Set 10

This practice set contains four writing tasks. These are described below.

Task 1: Short Passage with Questions

This task has a short passage followed by questions. Read each question carefully. Then write your answer in the space provided.

You can also practice writing skills by completing the Core Skills Practice exercise.

Task 2: Short Passage with Questions

This task has a short passage followed by questions. Read each question carefully. Then write your answer in the space provided.

You can also practice writing skills by completing the Core Skills Practice exercise.

Task 3: Short Story Writing Task

This task requires you to write a short story. Read the writing prompt, complete the planning page, and then write or type your answer.

Task 4: Opinion Piece Writing Task

This final task requires you to write an opinion piece. Read the writing prompt, complete the planning page, and then write or type your answer.

Task 1: Short Passage with Questions

Silver

Silver is a shiny metal. It is the best conductor of both heat and electricity. Even though it conducts electricity well, silver is not often used in wiring. Copper is used in wiring because it is far cheaper to buy. Silver is also the most reflective of all the metals. It is used in mirrors and other reflective coatings. It is also used in photographic film. Another use is in solar panels and electronic devices such as mobile phones.

Silver is often used to make jewelry, cutlery, and items like serving plates. Silver can even be used to sterilize water. This has been known for a very long time. The Persian king Cyrus the Great had his water supply boiled and sealed in silver vessels.

Silver Use in 2012

Use of Silver	Percent Used
Photography	15%
Jewelry	20%
Silverware	15%
Coins and Bars	5%
Industrial Uses	40%
Other	5%

Silver is also used to make coins and bars. Quarters, dimes, and nickels are not made from silver, but investors can buy coins and bars made of silver.

CORE SKILLS PRACTICE

Summarize the passage by listing **three** things that make silver special compared to other metals.

1. ______________________________

2. ______________________________

3. ______________________________

1 How is the information in the table important to the passage?

Hint

In your answer, describe what information is given in the table and how it relates to or expands on the information in the passage.

2 Even though silver is a good conductor of electricity, it is rarely used in wiring. Explain why.

Task 2: Short Passage with Questions

Camels

Camels can survive for long periods of time without drinking water. The camel's hump is a big help with this. But it does not actually store water. It stores fat. The fat is used as a source of energy. Many people forget that deserts are known for having little food as well as little water. By storing fat, camels can survive for weeks or even months without food. Camels do store water. They store it in their bodies and in their blood.

Camels can go longer than 7 days without drinking. When they do find water, they can take a lot in. They are able to consume over 50 gallons of water at a time! These features allow them to survive in the desert.

Camels were once found in North America. They are now mainly found in the deserts of the African and Arabian regions.

CORE SKILLS PRACTICE
WRITE A RESEARCH REPORT

There are many other plants and animals that are suited to desert conditions. Choose one of the plants or animals listed below. Research what features the plant or animal has that help it survive in the desert. Then write a report describing what you learned.

rattlesnake
Gila monster
prickly pear
saguaro cactus

1 How does a camel's hump help it survive?

2 Which details from the passage did you find most interesting?

Hint

This question is asking for your personal opinion. As well as describing what you found most interesting, make sure you also briefly explain why.

3 What features allow camels to survive in deserts? Use details from the passage in your answer.

Hint Focus on how the features of camels help them overcome the main problems of living in deserts.

Writing and Editing Checklist

After you finish writing your answer to question 3, you can use this guide to review and edit your work. Use the questions as a guide to finding ways you can improve your work.

Writing Checklist

- ✓ Does your work have a strong opening? Does it introduce the topic and the main ideas?
- ✓ Is your work well-organized? Is related information grouped together? Does each paragraph have one main idea?
- ✓ Have you clearly explained two or three features that help camels survive? Have you used details from the passage to support your claims?
- ✓ Is your work focused? Are there any details that do not fit with your main ideas?
- ✓ Do your ideas flow well? Have you used words and phrases to link ideas well?

Editing Checklist

- ✓ Have you used a variety of sentence structures? Are your sentences all written correctly?
- ✓ Is the grammar correct?
- ✓ Are all words spelled correctly? You can check the spelling of any words you are not sure of.
- ✓ Is punctuation used correctly?
- ✓ Are all words capitalized correctly?

Task 3: Short Story Writing Task

Directions: Read the writing prompt below. Use the planning page to plan your writing. Then write or type your answer.

Karen was ready to step out onto the stage. She was trying out for the school play. She really wanted to get a good part in the play.

Write a story about Karen and how she tries out for the school play.

Hint

One way to improve your writing is to focus on how you describe things. You can choose words and phrases that make your writing more interesting.

Imagine that you want to describe how nervous Karen felt before trying out. Instead of saying that she was nervous, you might describe how she paced back and forth. You can also use literary devices such as similes or hyperbole to add emphasis. For example, you could write that Karen paced back and forth so many times that she started to wear a hole in the stage.

By describing things in a more interesting way, you will make your story more interesting to the reader.

Planning Page

The Story
Write a summary of your story.

The Beginning
Describe what is going to happen at the start of your story.

The Middle
Describe what is going to happen in the middle of your story.

The End
Describe what is going to happen at the end of your story.

Task 4: Opinion Piece Writing Task

Directions: Read the writing prompt below. Use the planning page to plan your writing. Then write or type your answer.

Read this piece of advice.

> If you can solve your problem, then what is the need of worrying? If you cannot solve it, then what is the use of worrying?
> -Shantideva

Write an opinion piece in which you explain to people why there is no use worrying. Use facts, details, or examples in your answer.

Hint

Start by thinking about what the advice means. It means that if you can't solve a problem, worrying about it won't help. However, if you can solve a problem, then you should solve it so you don't have to worry. In your opinion piece, you should write an argument that persuades people that there is no use worrying.

You can use a specific example to make your argument clear and focused. Start by thinking of an example from your own life where you worried about something. For example, you could describe one situation where you worried a lot about something, and tell how worrying did not help. You could write about how you wished you had of solved the problem to avoid wasting all that time worrying.

If you can't think of an example from your own life, you can make up an example that readers will relate to. For example, you could describe a student worrying about a test instead of taking action and studying for it. Use one specific example from your own life or one specific example you make up as the basis of your argument.

Planning Page

Summary
Write a brief summary of what you are going to write about.

Supporting Details
Write down the facts, details, or examples you are going to include.

Outline
Write a plan for what you are going to write. Include the main points you want to cover and the order you will cover them.

Writing and Editing Checklist

After you finish writing your opinion piece, you can use this guide to review and edit your work. Use the questions as a guide to finding ways you can improve your work.

Writing Checklist

- ✓ Does your work have one clear opinion?
- ✓ Does your work have a strong opening? Does the opening introduce the topic and state the opinion?
- ✓ Is your opinion supported? Have you used facts, details, and examples to support your opinion?
- ✓ Is your work well-organized? Is related information grouped together? Does each paragraph have one main idea?
- ✓ Do your ideas flow well? Have you used words and phrases to link ideas well?
- ✓ Does your work have a strong ending? Does the ending restate the main idea and tie up the opinion piece?

Editing Checklist

- ✓ Have you used a variety of sentence structures? Are your sentences all written correctly?
- ✓ Is the grammar correct?
- ✓ Are all words spelled correctly? You can check the spelling of any words you are not sure of.
- ✓ Is punctuation used correctly?
- ✓ If dialogue is used, is it punctuated correctly?
- ✓ Are all words capitalized correctly?

Answer Key

Developing Writing Skills

Student learning in North Carolina is based on the skills described in the *North Carolina Standard Course of Study*. These standards were introduced in 2017, and fully implemented in the 2018-2019 school year. The standards describe what students are expected to know. This workbook is specifically designed to develop the writing skills described in the standards. Students will write in response to passages, as well as write narratives, persuasive texts, and essays. Students will gain experience completing research projects and edit and revise their work. While the workbook is mainly focused on writing skills, students will also develop strong reading skills as they provide written answers to reading comprehension questions.

Core Skills Practice Exercises

Each short passage in this workbook includes an exercise focused on one key writing, reading, or language skill described in the *North Carolina Standard Course of Study*. The answer key identifies the core skill covered by each exercise, and describes what to look for in the student's response.

Scoring Constructed-Response Questions

The short passages in this workbook include constructed-response questions, where students provide a written answer to a question. Short questions are scored out of 2 and longer questions are scored out of 4. The answer key gives guidance on how to score these questions. Use the criteria listed as a guide to scoring these questions, and as a guide for giving the student advice on how to improve an answer.

Scoring Writing Tasks

The writing tasks in this workbook are scored based on rubrics that list the features expected of student writing. These features are based on the state standards. The rubrics used for scoring these questions are included in the back of this book. Use the rubric to score these questions, and as a guide for giving the student advice on how to improve an answer.

Practice Set 1

Task 1: Short Passage with Questions (Mozart)

Core Skills Practice

Core skill: Write informative/explanatory texts to examine a topic and convey ideas and information clearly.

Answer: Use the Informative/Explanatory Writing Rubric to give a score out of 4.

Q1. Give a score of 0, 1, or 2 based on how many details are correctly given.

- The details may include that he composed over 600 pieces of music, wrote music for different instruments, wrote whole operas, or started composing music at age 5.

Q2. Give a score of 0, 1, or 2 based on how many pairs of places and details are correctly listed.

- Paris Searched for work / Wrote music
- Vienna Wrote his best-known work

Task 2: Short Passage with Questions (Clowns)

Core Skills Practice

Core skill: Determine a theme of a story, drama, or poem from details in the text, including how characters in a story or drama respond to challenges or how the speaker in a poem reflects upon a topic; summarize the text.

Answer: The student should describe how Mickey becomes less scared of clowns.

Q1. Give a score of 0, 1, or 2 based on how well the answer meets the criteria listed.

- It should identify Mickey's main problem as being that he is afraid of clowns.
- It should describe how he overcomes the problem by facing his fear.

Q2. Give a score of 0, 1, or 2 based on how well the answer meets the criteria listed.

- It should identify that the word "pranced" indicates how the clowns moved.
- It should tell how the word "pranced" implies that the clowns bounded about, moved with energy, or moved in a joyful way.

Task 3: Long Passage with Essay Question

Use the Informative/Explanatory Writing Rubric to review the work and give a score out of 4.

Task 4: Personal Narrative Writing Task

Use the Narrative Writing Rubric to review the work and give a score out of 4.

Practice Set 2

Task 1: Short Passage with Questions (Raindrops)

Core Skills Practice

Core skill: Determine two or more main ideas of a text and explain how they are supported by key details; summarize the text.

Answer: The student should identify the main idea of the first paragraph as being about how people think raindrops are shaped, and the main idea of the second paragraph as being about how raindrops are actually shaped.

Q1. Give a score of 0, 1, or 2 based on how well the answer meets the criteria listed.
- It should describe how the diagram shows that raindrops are often shown to look like tears.
- It may describe the diagram as an example of how weather reports often show raindrops.

Q2. Give a score of 0, 1, or 2 based on how well the answer meets the criteria listed.
- It should compare the actual shape of raindrops with the mistaken shape of raindrops.
- It should describe how raindrops are spherical, but are mistaken as being teardrop-shaped.

Task 2: Short Passage with Questions (Dearest Donna)

Core Skills Practice

Core skill: Use digital tools and resources to produce and publish writing as well as to interact and collaborate with others.

Answer: The student should write a poem of four lines where the second and fourth lines rhyme.

Q1. Give a score of 0, 1, or 2 based on how well the answer meets the criteria listed.
- It may state that each verse has two pairs of rhyming lines.
- It may state that in each verse, lines 1 and 2 rhyme and lines 3 and 4 rhyme.

Q2. Give a score of 0, 1, or 2 based on how well the answer meets the criteria listed.
- It should identify that the poem is addressed to Donna, or to the speaker's girlfriend.
- It should give evidence to support this. The evidence referred to could include the title of the poem, the use of "you" and "we," or the message of the poem.

Task 3: Short Story Writing Task

Use the Narrative Writing Rubric to review the work and give a score out of 4.

Task 4: Opinion Piece Writing Task

Use the Opinion Writing Rubric to review the work and give a score out of 4.

Practice Set 3

Task 1: Short Passage with Questions (Something Special)

Core Skills Practice

Core skill: Write opinion pieces on topics or texts, supporting a point of view with reasons and information.

Answer: Use the Opinion Writing Rubric to review the work and give a score out of 4.

Q1. Give a score of 0, 1, or 2 based on how many correct ways are given. Possible answer are listed.

- Playing on weekends with friends, playing by himself after school, practicing his ball skills

Q2. Give a score of 0, 1, or 2 based on how well the answer meets the criteria listed.

- It should explain that Toby improved his ball skills while practicing alone.
- It should describe how Toby's coach selected him because of his ball skills.

Task 2: Short Passage with Questions (Penny's Powers)

Core Skills Practice

Core skill: Quote accurately from a text when explaining what the text says explicitly and when drawing inferences from the text.

Answer: The student should explain that Penny is not selfish. The answer should show an understanding that she does not use her powers because she does not realize that other people need things.

Q1. Give a score of 0, 1, or 2 based on how well the answer meets the criteria listed.

- The answer should focus on how Penny has magic wishing powers that could not really exist.

Q2. Give a score of 0, 1, or 2 based on how well the answer meets the criteria listed.

- It should identify the hyperbole as when the castle is described as almost reaching the clouds.
- The purpose could be emphasizing the height of the castle, or creating a sense of wonder.

Q3. Give a score of 0, 1, 2, 3, or 4 based on how well the answer meets the criteria listed.

- It should tell how Penny realizes she is lucky, or realizes she can use her powers for good.
- It should describe how meeting the poor man makes Penny realize that she should help others.
- It may refer to how pleased and grateful the man is, or may infer that Penny wants to make others feel the same joy as the poor man.

Task 3: Long Passage with Essay Question

Use the Informative/Explanatory Writing Rubric to review the work and give a score out of 4.

Task 4: Personal Narrative Writing Task

Use the Narrative Writing Rubric to review the work and give a score out of 4.

Practice Set 4

Task 1: Short Passage with Questions (Brain Size)

Core Skills Practice

Core skill: Conduct short research projects that use several sources to build knowledge through investigation of different aspects of a topic.

Answer: The student should research how ants communicate with each other, and write a short description of how ants communicate.

Q1. Give a score of 0, 1, or 2 based on how well the answer meets the criteria listed.

- It may describe how the author wants readers to think about the topic, or how the author wants readers to be curious or interested.

Q2. Give a score of 0, 1, or 2 based on how many facts are listed. Possible answers are listed.

- Ants have the largest brain size in relation to its size. The brain of an ant is 6 percent of body weight. The brain of a human is 2 percent of body weight. An average nest has 40,000 ants.

Task 2: Short Passage with Questions (Mosquitoes)

Core Skills Practice

Core skill: Conduct short research projects that use several sources to build knowledge through investigation of different aspects of a topic.

Answer: The diseases listed could include West Nile virus, Dengue fever, Yellow fever, Ross River fever, and St. Louis Encephalitis.

Q1. Give a score of 0, 1, or 2 based on how well the answer meets the criteria listed.

- It should make a reasonable prediction of what another sentence would describe.
- The prediction should relate to Patrick Manson's research.

Q2. Give a score of 0, 1, or 2 based on how well the answer meets the criteria listed.

- It should identify one similarity, such as that both male and female mosquitoes carry diseases.
- It should identify one difference, such as that only female mosquitoes bite humans or that male mosquitoes do not pass on diseases.

Task 3: Opinion Piece Writing Task

Use the Opinion Writing Rubric to review the work and give a score out of 4.

Task 4: Short Story Writing Task

Use the Narrative Writing Rubric to review the work and give a score out of 4.

Practice Set 5

Task 1: Short Passage with Questions (The Olympics)

Core Skills Practice

Core skill: Write informative/explanatory texts to examine a topic and convey ideas and information clearly.

Answer: Use the Informative/Explanatory Writing Rubric to give a score out of 4.

Q1. Give a score of 0, 1, or 2 based on how many facts or opinions are correctly listed.

- The facts could include that the Olympics are global, feature indoor or outdoor sports, have summer and winter versions, are held every 4 years, or were first held in 1896.
- The opinions listed could include that they are enjoyed by people all over the world, that they are an important event, or that they bring people from all countries together.

Q2. Give a score of 0, 1, or 2 based on how well the answer meets the criteria listed.

- It should give a supported opinion on why the Olympics are popular.
- It may include supporting details, or may be based on the student's own ideas or experiences.

Task 2: Short Passage with Questions (The Light)

Core Skills Practice

Core skill: Write narratives to develop real or imagined experiences or events.

Answer: The student should write a description of the events from Christopher's point of view.

Q1. Give a score of 0, 1, or 2 based on how well the answer meets the criteria listed.

- It should refer to how the author describes the light.
- It may refer to the imagery used or to specific words used like *shimmer* and *dazzling*.

Q2. Give a score of 0, 1, or 2 based on how well the answer meets the criteria listed.

- It should state whether Christopher feels afraid or curious.
- Either answer is acceptable, as long as it includes an explanation to support the opinion.

Q3. Give a score of 0, 1, 2, 3, or 4 based on how well the answer meets the criteria listed.

- It should draw a valid conclusion about what the light is.
- It should make a valid prediction about what will happen next.

Task 3: Long Passage with Essay Question

Use the Informative/Explanatory Writing Rubric to review the work and give a score out of 4.

Task 4: Explanatory Writing Task

Use the Informative/Explanatory Writing Rubric to review the work and give a score out of 4.

Practice Set 6

Task 1: Short Passage with Questions (Peace and Not War)

Core Skills Practice

Core skill: Write narratives to develop real or imagined experiences or events.

Answer: The student should describe an argument he or she had with something. The answer should include who was argued with and what was argued about.

Q1. Give a score of 0, 1, or 2 based on how well the answer meets the criteria listed.

- It should explain that Terry and Mark both want to watch different things on the television.
- It may specify that Mark hates football, while Terry hates cartoons.

Q2. Give a score of 0, 1, or 2 based on how well the answer meets the criteria listed.

- It should explain that the lounge room sounding like a zoo shows how loud and chaotic it sounded.
- It may expand on this to suggest that describing the lounge room this way suggests that Terry and Mark were acting like animals.

Task 2: Short Passage with Questions (The Dodo)

Core Skills Practice

Core skill: Write informative/explanatory texts to examine a topic and convey ideas and information clearly.

Answer: Use the Informative/Explanatory Writing Rubric to give a score out of 4.

Q1. Give a score of 0, 1, or 2 based on how well the answer meets the criteria listed.

- It should identify that the common phrase is "as dead as a dodo."
- It should explain that the phrase means that something is gone forever.

Q2. Give a score of 0, 1, or 2 based on how many correct reasons are given.

- The reasons listed could include that dodos build their nests on the ground, that ground-based animals ate the eggs, that people hunted dodos for meat, or that forest habitats were destroyed.

Task 3: Short Story Writing Task

Use the Narrative Writing Rubric to review the work and give a score out of 4.

Task 4: Opinion Piece Writing Task

Use the Opinion Writing Rubric to review the work and give a score out of 4.

Practice Set 7

Task 1: Short Passage with Questions (Letter to the Editor)

Core Skills Practice

Core skill: Write opinion pieces on topics or texts, supporting a point of view with reasons and information.

Answer: The student should write a paragraph giving an opinion on how the problems in the town park could be solved. The solutions should be relevant, reasonable, and clearly explained.

Q1. Give a score of 0, 1, or 2 based on how many examples are correctly given.

- The examples should be cans and broken glass.

Q2. Give a score of 0, 1, or 2 based on how well the answer meets the criteria listed.

- It should explain how Evan could improve his argument.
- It may describe how Evan could give more details, how Evan could use imagery, how Evan could compare the park to how it once was, or any other reasonable method for making the state of the park clearer to the reader.

Task 2: Short Passage with Questions (Tom's Time Machine)

Core Skills Practice

Core skill: Write narratives to develop real or imagined experiences or events.

Answer: Use the Narrative Writing Rubric to review the work and give a score out of 4.

Q1. Give a score of 0, 1, or 2 based on how well the answer meets the criteria listed.

- It should circle one of the words. Any of the words could be reasonable answers, as long as the choice is supported.
- It should include a reasonable and well-supported explanation of why the student chose that word.

Q2. Give a score of 0, 1, or 2 based on how well the answer meets the criteria listed.

- It should identify the genre as science fiction.
- It should give relevant evidence. The evidence could be specific, such as stating that the passage involves time travel. The evidence could be general, such as stating that the passage involves things that are not possible now and that it involves science.

Task 3: Long Passage with Essay Question

Use the Informative/Explanatory Writing Rubric to review the work and give a score out of 4.

Task 4: Personal Narrative Writing Task

Use the Narrative Writing Rubric to review the work and give a score out of 4.

Practice Set 8

Task 1: Short Passage with Questions (Sugar)

Core Skills Practice

Core skill: Write informative/explanatory texts to examine a topic and convey ideas and information clearly.

Answer: Use the Informative/Explanatory Writing Rubric to give a score out of 4.

Q1. Give a score of 0, 1, or 2 based on how well the answer meets the criteria listed.
- It should list two facts or details about sugar given in the passage.
- The information should be paraphrased and not written exactly as stated in the passage.

Q2. Give a score of 0, 1, or 2 based on how well the answer meets the criteria listed.
- It should describe how sugar should be heated without water for it to caramelize.

Task 2: Short Passage with Questions (Creature Comforts)

Core Skills Practice

Core skill: Write opinion pieces on topics or texts, supporting a point of view with reasons and information.

Answer: The student should give an opinion on whether or not he or she would enjoy being a farmer, and should support the opinion with a valid explanation.

Q1. Give a score of 0, 1, or 2 based on how well the answer meets the criteria listed.
- It should identify that the theme is about caring for animals, living a simple life, or enjoying what you do.

Q2. Give a score of 0, 1, or 2 based on how well the answer meets the criteria listed.
- It should tell how personification is used when the wind is described as trying to annoy Fred.
- It should draw a valid conclusion about the purpose of the personification. The purpose could be to make the wind seem real, or to suggest that Fred was battling the elements.

Q3. Give a score of 0, 1, 2, 3, or 4 based on how well the answer meets the criteria listed.
- It should make a valid inference about what matters most to Fred.
- It should refer to how Fred cares about taking care of his farm and animals.
- It should use relevant supporting details from the passage.

Task 3: Opinion Piece Writing Task

Use the Opinion Writing Rubric to review the work and give a score out of 4.

Task 4: Short Story Writing Task

Use the Narrative Writing Rubric to review the work and give a score out of 4.

Practice Set 9

Task 1: Short Passage with Questions (Herbal Tea)

Core Skills Practice

Core skill: Conduct short research projects that use several sources to build knowledge through investigation of different aspects of a topic.

Answer: The student should complete the chart with one benefit of peppermint tea and one benefit of chamomile tea. Benefits of peppermint tea include aiding digestion, relieving headaches, and treating colds. Benefits of chamomile tea include reducing stress and helping people sleep.

Q1. Give a score of 0, 1, or 2 based on how well the answer meets the criteria listed.

- It should explain that the main purpose of the passage is to instruct or to teach readers how to do something.

Q2. Give a score of 0, 1, or 2 based on how many correct actions are listed.

- The optional actions include adding sugar, letting the tea sit for longer than 30 seconds, adding milk or cream, and using a teapot instead of a cup.

Task 2: Short Passage with Questions (A Day in the Life)

Core Skills Practice

Core skill: Write narratives to develop real or imagined experiences or events.

Answer: Use the Narrative Writing Rubric to review the work and give a score out of 4.

Q1. Give a score of 0, 1, or 2 based on how many activities are correctly listed.

- The activities listed should be doing paperwork, pulling over speeding people, tracking down thieves, and directing traffic.

Q2. Give a score of 0, 1, or 2 based on how well the answer meets the criteria listed.

- It should clearly explain the relevance of the passage's title.
- It should refer to how the passage describes what a police officer does on a day at work.

Task 3: Long Passage with Essay Question

Use the Informative/Explanatory Writing Rubric to review the work and give a score out of 4.

Task 4: Explanatory Writing Task

Use the Informative/Explanatory Writing Rubric to review the work and give a score out of 4.

Practice Set 10

Task 1: Short Passage with Questions (Silver)

Core Skills Practice

Core skill: Quote accurately from a text when explaining what the text says explicitly and when drawing inferences from the text.

Answer: The student may describe how silver conducts heat better than other metals, conducts electricity better than other metals, is the most reflective metal, or how it sterilizes water.

Q1. Give a score of 0, 1, or 2 based on how well the answer meets the criteria listed.

- It should explain that the table gives specific information on how much silver is used for different purposes.

Q2. Give a score of 0, 1, or 2 based on how well the answer meets the criteria listed.

- It should explain that silver is not used because it is too expensive, or that copper is used instead because it is much cheaper.

Task 2: Short Passage with Questions (Camels)

Core Skills Practice

Core skill: Write informative/explanatory texts to examine a topic and convey ideas and information clearly.

Answer: Use the Informative/Explanatory Writing Rubric to give a score out of 4.

Q1. Give a score of 0, 1, or 2 based on how well the answer meets the criteria listed.

- It should explain how a camel's hump helps it survive.
- It should refer to how a camel's hump stores fat, and how the camel can use the fat for energy.

Q2. Give a score of 0, 1, or 2 based on how well the answer meets the criteria listed.

- It should identify details from the passage that the student found interesting.
- It should include a brief explanation of why the student found the details interesting.

Q3. Give a score of 0, 1, 2, 3, or 4 based on how well the answer meets the criteria listed.

- It should describe some features of camels that help them survive in deserts.
- It should refer to how a camel's hump stores fat that can be used for energy.
- It may also describe how camels can store water in their bodies and blood, or how camels can take in a lot of water and then go for days without drinking.

Task 3: Short Story Writing Task

Use the Narrative Writing Rubric to review the work and give a score out of 4.

Task 4: Opinion Piece Writing Task

Use the Opinion Writing Rubric to review the work and give a score out of 4.

INFORMATIVE/EXPLANATORY WRITING RUBRIC

This writing rubric is based on the state standards and describes the features that are expected in student writing. Give students a score out of 4 based on how well the answer meets the criteria. Then average the scores to give a total score out of 4. Students can also be given feedback and guidance based on the criteria below.

	Score	Notes
Organization and Purpose To receive a full score, the response will: • have an opening that introduces the topic • have a clear focus • be well-organized with related information grouped together • include formatting such as headings when appropriate • provide a concluding statement or section		
Evidence and Elaboration To receive a full score, the response will: • develop the topic with facts, details, quotations, or examples • include relevant text-based evidence when appropriate		
Written Expression To receive a full score, the response will: • be clear and easy to understand • have good transitions between ideas • use language to communicate ideas effectively		
Writing Conventions To receive a full score, the response will: • have few or no spelling errors • have few or no grammar errors • have few or no capitalization errors • have few or no punctuation errors		
Total Score		

OPINION WRITING RUBRIC

This writing rubric is based on the state standards and describes the features that are expected in student writing. Give students a score out of 4 based on how well the answer meets the criteria. Then average the scores to give a total score out of 4. Students can also be given feedback and guidance based on the criteria below.

	Score	Notes
Organization and Purpose To receive a full score, the response will: • have an opening that introduces the topic and states an opinion • have a clear focus • be well-organized with related information grouped together • provide a concluding statement or section		
Evidence and Elaboration To receive a full score, the response will: • provide reasons to support the opinion • develop the topic with facts, details, or examples • include relevant text-based evidence when appropriate		
Written Expression To receive a full score, the response will: • be clear and easy to understand • have good transitions between ideas • use language to communicate ideas effectively		
Writing Conventions To receive a full score, the response will: • have few or no spelling errors • have few or no grammar errors • have few or no capitalization errors • have few or no punctuation errors		
Total Score		

NARRATIVE WRITING RUBRIC

This writing rubric is based on the state standards and describes the features that are expected in student writing. Give students a score out of 4 based on how well the answer meets the criteria. Then average the scores to give a total score out of 4. Students can also be given feedback and guidance based on the criteria below.

	Score	Notes
Organization and Purpose To receive a full score, the response will: • have an effective opening that introduces the situation, characters, or event • have a logical and organized event sequence • have an effective ending		
Development and Elaboration To receive a full score, the response will: • have clearly developed characters, setting, and events • use dialogue and descriptions effectively • use concrete words and sensory details • use narrative techniques effectively • have an appropriate style		
Written Expression To receive a full score, the response will: • be clear and easy to understand • have good transitions between ideas • use language to communicate ideas effectively		
Writing Conventions To receive a full score, the response will: • have few or no spelling errors • have few or no grammar errors • have few or no capitalization errors • have few or no punctuation errors		
Total Score		

Made in the USA
Columbia, SC
22 June 2022